VRITRAHAN

त्वमेकस्य वृत्रहन्नविता द्वयोरसि । उतेदृशे यथा वयम् ॥

Rig Veda 6.45.5

Advance Praise

'This is a remarkable work of poetry—ingenious and lyrical. Though titled "Vritrahan", it is much more than that. It is steeped in adhyatma and dharma and has a mystical quality that transcends the Vritra story. Ratul Chakraborty's voice is one that deserves to be heard and read more and more.'

Bibek Debroy, writer and economist

'Here is Ratul's "mad" project to single-handedly revive the ancient Indian tradition of composing epics and the telling of sacred mythology in grand verse. The idea is to bring back the magical and evoke a feeling of wonder at the universe, and Ratul does it with a retelling of Indra's slaying of the dragon Vritra.'

Sanjeev Sanyal, writer and economist

VRITRAHAN

Ratul Chakraborty

ink | OCCAM

ISBN: 978-93-6547-822-8

First published in India 2025
This edition published 2025

BluOne Ink Pvt. Ltd
A-76, 2nd Floor, Sector 136, Noida
Uttar Pradesh 201301
www.bluone.ink
publisher@bluone.ink

Printed and bound in India at Nutech Print Services - India

For the victims of the partition of Bharat in 1947

and

In memory of Dr Bibek Debroy and Gogo

CONTENTS

ACKNOWLEDGEMENTS

This is the maddest thing I have ever done.

I had very little belief in my ability to write this book. That impossible journey was made possible with the support of many gentle souls. *Vritrahan* is the fruit of their kindness.

First and foremost, I bow down to Bharat Mata and her rishis. May I have the good fortune to play in Her lap in all my future lives as well.

I wish to acknowledge the maestro Swargiya Shri Ishiro Honda for *Gojira* (1954), which left an indelible mark on my creative consciousness when I first watched it more than two decades ago.

My friend Shri Raghava Krishna has suffered (and has been suffering for years) the brunt of my creative churn. His sparkling moral clarity coupled with his inexhaustible kindness has been an ever-present beacon of support from the moment I first met him. Thank you for everything, Raghava.

This book could not have been written without the love and generosity of Shri Hari Kiran Vadlamani and the Indic Academy. I am extremely grateful for his kindness, for the faith he has shown in my limited abilities as well as his patience at being bombarded by random WhatsApp messages containing unfinished excerpts, often without any context. Thank you, sir – it is my honour and privilege that this work is blessed by its association with IndicA.

I would like to thank Smt. Jennifer Mcgee, Shri Deepak M.R., Shri Pranshu B. Saxena, Shri Neelabh Pratap Singh, Shri Shivakumar G.V., Smt. Saiswaroopa Iyer, and Shri Abhinav Agarwal for their invaluable feedback and support during the writing process. Your words were the fuel that stopped me from giving up in self-doubt.

I would like to express my gratitude to Swargiya Dr Bibek Debroy for sharing his insights after reading through the manuscript. I will never forget his gentle words of encouragement and the immense support he gave to this book.

I would like to thank Shri Sanjeev Sanyal for his feedback and support towards this book.

I am grateful to Dr Nagaraj Paturi for the illuminating telephone conversations we had when this book was still at a concept stage. His words and works have been a guiding light for me.

I would also like to thank Dr S. Kalyanaraman and Dr Bharat Gupt for the treasure trove of knowledge they have shared with us through their books, papers, and talks, all of which have helped me immensely in the creation of this work.

I thank my wonderful parents-in-law, Shri Ashoke Mukhopadhyay and Smt. Shovona Mukherjee, for the constant encouragement they have given me and the enriching conversations we frequently have.

Thank you, Ma and Baba, for everything.

Thank you, Gogo, Truffles, and Mowgli, for blessing our family with your unconditional love.

Finally, thank you, Titli, for enduring all the ups and downs with me. Your kindness, understanding, and belief have made all of this possible.

This ignorant one submits all his feeble efforts at the feet of Ma Saraswati and seeks refuge in Her infinite grace.

AUTHOR'S NOTE

Indic untranslatables have been used wherever necessary to maintain the flow and the authenticity of the narration. Footnotes and chapter endnotes have been omitted for the same reason. The Sutradhar begs your indulgence in this matter.

A CONFESSION, A CAVEAT, AND A WARNING

This is your story.

Everything that happens in the following pages has been experienced by you or will be. I am just the chronicler, the Sutradhar.

Actually, no.

To be completely honest, the truth is, I am… you.

Sorry, there was no gentler way to break this.

I am you.

Your voice. Your thoughts. You yourself, no matter who or what or where you are at this precise moment – know that you are also here in this tale.

Because this is your story too. Yours, mine… ours.

This is how it all began.

Just before my death, I found myself stranded alone on the asphalt ribbon that bisected an endless desert. It hardly mattered to me how or why I was in this situation – I am sure you will agree that recent events are ample proof that most of the important stuff, small or large, are hardly ever in our control; assuming anything else is foolishness.

To the west, I could see the Temple of Ashapura Devi which I remembered visiting… some time ago. From the east, I felt an immense emptiness rushing towards me.

The ground shook. Lightning flashed across the darkened horizon, illuminating the frothing pillars of dust that seethed in rage towards the roiling sky. The wind howled as if jackals in frenzy, hurling sharp shards of grit like the relentless pangs of guilt in a novice human.

Overcome by mortal terror, I began to run towards the temple. The sound of bells reached out to me like a fool's hope, briefly rising above the onrushing storm before getting consumed by rumbling thunder.

And then I witnessed Her.

Her form, the radiant darkness of the void.

Her hair spread out in waves, covering the sky.

Her steps submerged the earth in blood.

Her breath was the onyx fear which froze all senses.

Her *Darshan, surrender.*

Could I be so lucky?

I fell on my knees and wept like a newborn.

Her eyes were filled with infinite love as she chopped my head off and placed it in her garland.

That is how we met, neighbour.

PART ONE

ORIGINS

The Sutradhar appears, wearing the mask of a *changing constellation*.

01 SEEKING GRACE

The Sutradhar Speaks

To Her lotus feet lead all paths
With Her rests all the mysteries which seekers seek
In Her benevolence the lost ones discover
The gateway to the ocean of Bliss.

Home.
I am at your doorstep again,
Reduced to nothing but a tired stray;
Let me rest a while, Mother.

No more do I want to climb the heights.
Let me be a *Kusha* stalk, Mother,
Content,
Sufficient,
Wedded to the wet earth of this land;
After all, what else is of value,
But this fragrant petrichor,
Promise of life eternal?

Yet, can mere existence be enough,
For one who aspires to be a worthy son?

Unthinking of fame and fortune,
Unmindful of taunts and derision,
I must set out on yet another journey
Far beyond my capacity.

Permit this wretched one
To undertake a penance,
To atone my deeds
And warn my peers;
Let me record the tale
Of the fall of Heaven's King,
The path to his redemption
And the unity he forged.

A Prayer to Ma Saraswati (*The Sutradhar*)

I bow to you, Mother of the universe!
O supreme Goddess, the essence of purity!
O Saraswati, the fount of all wisdom!
O Vak Devi who makes us *Aarya*!
O Mother Bharati cradling *Dharma*!
O Mother, Mother, Mother,
Hear my plea!

Once more indulge your undeserving child.
Grant me your favour.
Let essence overflow my veins.
May sapience temper my foolish passions.
Guide my witless self on this quest,
Bestow upon my pen your boon,
An infinitesimal fragment of Grace –
That priceless fuel of metamorphosis
Which turned the terrifying robber into the first poet.

Let this humble offering become a pebble,
Immersed in the riverbed of your nectar stream
Picked up by those who seek,
Passed on to those they love.

1| THE WHEEL TURNS

The Sutradhar Speaks

Shiva,
The Supreme God,
Opened His *Third Eye*;
Obeying His will,
The Wheel of Time stopped turning.

On that last day of existence
The infinite beats of a *damaru*
Resonated through the firmament.
Fear possessed all;
The world was submerged
In pitiful terror.

The Daughter of the World looked up.
Seven terrible suns blazed across the sky
Resplendent, night-banishing;
By the edge of the western sea
She began the dance of *Pralaya*
To the rhythm of *Adi Tala.*

When She danced
The world held its breath
For a single moment
Which seemed to stretch forever,
Until the clouds parted

To reveal the prancing *Uchchaihshravas*,
That seven-headed white horse
Gleaming, flawless, perfect in form
Finally unbound from Heaven's service.

From deep within the churning depths,
Snorting, untamed, and wild
Shrieking to the skies
Rose the Emerald Mare.

Boundless desire shimmered in her belly;
Resplendent under the crimson doomlight
She drew in *Uchchaihshravas*
To unite amidst the frothing waves.

From that coupling emerged an inferno.

The dazzling green *Vadava* spiralled out,
Bearing the face of the Mare in throes of ecstasy;
That irrepressible submarine fire
All destroying,
All consuming,
Began to engulf the universe
Filling up the spaces between the stars and the atoms –
The music of the spheres went silent
Announcing the onset of *Rudra Tandava*.

Mounting the white stallion
She who was at once Janaki and Parvati
Galloped across the collapsing reality
In search of the Secret Gate,
Lotus shaped and golden-hued.

In Her wake,
A lament rose in countless voices
Despair seeped across galaxies –
Fuel to the rampaging firestorm
Thunder to the furious lightning.

Then the ur-rain fell from the absent sky
Drowning that fresh nothingness
With the pristine stillness of the void;
The final peace flowered –
Soothing,
Calming,
No more fires,
No more lightning,
Just a shroud of mourning
Across the deep, aching, infinite silence.

That which had taken form
That which remained formless,
That which was living
That which had died,

That which was divine
That which was mundane,
Indeed, all things
Past, present, and those yet to be
Ceased to exist.

Only the ur-rain fell,
And kept falling-
No crops,
No deluge,
No *Malhar*,
Just an infinite descent
Until each bead shattered into mist.

Have you ever considered
The unfathomable sorrow of raindrops
With no earth to fall to?

In the centre of that non-existence
The Daughter of the World dismounted,
With a kiss on his forehead
She bade farewell to *Ucchaishraivas*.

The Stallion turned back.

Hiding his tears,
He trotted away with a lonesome gait,

Neighing with the sorrow
Of journey's end,
Until he lost himself in the empty cosmos.

Finally, alone,
The Daughter meditated
Commanding the Sacred Gate to take birth
From the Golden Womb of possibilities –
Hiranyagarbha.

2| TRUTH WITHIN THE LOTUS

The Sutradhar Speaks

The Golden Womb,
Hiranyagarbha
Exists.
That unique source,
That eternal cause,
Exists.

That which cannot be created
Nor manifested
Nor found
But that which simply is
The beginning of all things,
Hiranyagarbha.

Who has seen its cosmic hue?
Who has heard its infinite rhythm?
Who has felt its throbbing pulse?
The *Rishis* did.
They knew the Secrets.
They beheld the Truth.
The *Rishis* understood *Rta.*
Those great ones have declared,
Hiranyagarbha exists.
Because Hiranyagarbha exists
Everything exists –
Even all those things that don't.

Those countless stars exist.
The Sun and the Moon exist.
Our world exists.
This blade of grass exists.
That speck of dirt exists.
A drop of rain exists.
Warm bodies exist,
The bones of history exist.
The spark of action exists.
This time, this ... *now*, exists.

We too exist.
You and I.
In things said and left unsaid
In your breath and in my breath
In secret and in the open,
In whispers and joyous songs
Can you not feel the presence of *Hiranyagarbha*?

A mother's pain
The barren deserts
The lonely roads
The endless ocean
The teeming cities
The beehive and the termite mound
Cosmic dust and nuclear fire
The *ghee* for the *Yajna*

A sandalwood funeral pyre
Rotting, decaying corpses
Green shoots erupting
The fossil imprints on shale
The endless spiral
Of things Seen and Unseen,
Real and Imaginary,
And all that is in between them,
Is born in the *Hiranyagarbha*
And dies within it too.

Drawing upon the *Shakti* within Herself
The Daughter of the World manifested *Hiranyagarbha*
Out of the Nothingness of the Cosmic Void;
Or perhaps the *Hiranyagarbha* was already present
Waiting for the call of that *Shakti* –
Who can tell if it was this way or that
Or perhaps, even this way *and* that?

The *Hiranyagarbha* is the golden-hued egg;
It is also a lotus
The sound of OM
An old banyan tree,
Leaves casting shadow
On the reflections of stars
The *Hiranyagarbha* is all that is timeless,
Waiting within an altar unlit.

With Her last breath
The Daughter of the World
Lit the altar of ever-changing shapes.

She became the Mother.

3| SAMSARA

The Sutradhar Speaks

The vast empty nothingness
Which once was reality
Collapsed in on itself,
Shrinking, until it was no more
But a jewel between Her eyes.

Whispering the Mantra of Creation
To the flickering flame
The Mother offered that shining husk
Of all that was, and would have been –
An oblation of the spent universe
To kindle the primordial ritual;
Nothing else remained.
Just the *Yajna* and the Mother
Two points outside of space, time, and matter.

Answering the Mother's call
Shiva,
Supreme God,
Then revealed Himself
As both *Yoga* and *Yogi*;
Driven by His manifest will,
The Wheel of Time spun once more.

Then fire was created in the altar,
And existence came into existence, again.

Finally, the infant *Aatman* emerged
The precious fruit of the *Yajna*,
Naked,
Shivering,
Paralyzed in fear,
Crying helplessly
While the fresh shoots of a new reality
Shyly sprouted all around its ethereal shapelessness.

A Lament for Rebirth (*The Aatman*)

Again, I find myself bound alone
To this most unjust of yokes,
Life.
Merciless God,
Ever tormenting,
Drunk with the lust for creation
Are you not yet sated?

Never did I ask for life,
Never did I ask to be born,
Never did I agree to your cruel game,
Yet why must I be chained
To this inescapable spiral of rebirth?

If you are all-powerful, Mother,
Release me from the cycle

Let me pass away to blessed nothingness;
Or are you too a tyrant
Behind your loving smile and kindly face?

The Sutradhar Speaks

Bitterly did the *Aatman* weep
Cursing its very existence;
Consumed by helpless rage
It refused to be born
Until the Mother,
Highest *Guru*, ever loving,
Consoled Her errant child
Through gentle words of wisdom.

Remember Yourself (*The Mother*)

There is no God but you,
Forgetful child!

You are the Infinite potential
The maker and unmaker
The one consciousness
The eye of the storm
The mind which dreams
The first desire
The playful action

The supreme origin
The heart of creation
The only reality –
You are *Brahman*.

You, yes you, are the Universe,
From this grain of sand
To that exploding supernova
All will be you
And you will be all.

Why then do you weep,
When all life is but a tapestry
Connected by you,
Which is you,
Woven by you,
On a canvas
That is also you?

The Sutradhar Speaks

Purified by the fire in the Mother's words
The *Aatman*,
Who is the *Brahman*,
The free-est will
Established Two Laws
Karma and *The Cycle of Rebirth*
To serve as guides to the truest truth.

The Mother smiled,
Then did what had to be done
For the cosmic play to begin again,
Just as it had happened countless times before –
She wiped the slate clean.

The Aatman forgot everything.

A new reality was born,
Bursting with life
Divine and mortal
Each one of them the *Aatman* –
Born ignorant of their nature
Yet just one step away
From walking the path of *Yoga*,
To wake up and see,
The sublime joy beyond life and death
Resplendent, most beautiful.

Such is the journey of births
The crucible of mortality distilling our nature
Life after life,
Death after death,
Closer and closer to that state of purest bliss,
Ananda,
Until the Many finds the One
Until the Aatman meets the Brahman
And knows they were the same all along.

Discarding chains
Breaking limits
The joy of ascension
Losing oneself
Becoming everything,
Throbbing with the eternal rhythm of life –
Tell me, Is there anything more glorious?

But then again,
Decay too is the nature of things.

Aeons passed
Inertia crept in the darkness
Right and wrong tangled hopelessly
Systems collapsed;
The harmony promised by Dharma grew distorted
Contradictions gnawed at the seams of the world,
The taint of the emerging decay unsparing –
To those who had drunk the *Amrita*
And to those who hadn't.

Slowly did the shadows converge,
Pregnant with crisis;
The Age of Vritra was upon us.

PART TWO

ANTEBELLUM

The Sutradhar wears the mask of *distant thunder*.

1| A GOSSAMER SCAR

The Sutradhar Speaks

Three newborn birds,
Kapinjala, Kalapinga, and Tittiri,
Lay dying on a bed of red snow
In front of a destroyed altar
And the decapitated body
Of a three-headed man.

Their piteous titters
Though scarcely audible,
Echoed around that hermitage,
Cloaked in swirling sorrow and howling rage,
High on the icy Himalayas.

A shadow fell on the crying ones;
A giant hand scooped them up
Gentle, full of mercy
Fingers calloused yet delicate
Warm and comforting –
A place of refuge.

The newborn three looked up,
And saw a bearded face
Wrinkled with age
Overflowing with kindness,
Streaked with tears.

Using the light from the setting sun
He fashioned a golden nest
Which floated gently by his shoulders;
Cocooned in its warmth,
The chicks slept within.

Then the Old Man turned around,
And with heavy steps
Trudged to the sprawling carcass
Of what was once his son.

He sat weeping
With his child's torso on his lap;
His tears froze on that icebound peak
Then melted by his fiery grief
Dripped down from his white beard
As snowflakes made of sorrow.

Lament for a Son (*Old Man*)

Oh, Trishira! Oh my son!
You were wise. You had studied.
You spoke with intelligence.
You acted with compassion.

Oh, three-headed son of mine!
You could at once drink *Soma*,

Recite the *Vedas*,
Observe the world.

They called you *Vishvarupa* –
All the forms of this world,
Seen and unseen,
Were visible to you.

Yes, you were *Vishvarupa* –
Within you one could perceive,
All the forms of this world,
Seen and unseen.

Unshakeable in your vows
Fierce in your austerities
You foiled the jealous *Devatas*
And pleased the glorious Trinity.

Yet now you have passed.

Is there any act,
Which torments more
Than a father
Lighting his son's pyre?

Is there any path
More lonely,

Than that of a departing son
Trudging to Yama's abode?

Is there any mind,
More despairing,
Than those of the parents
Who has lost their child?

The Sutradhar Speaks

Thus, overcome by emotions,
The Old Man hugged the headless corpse.
He shed incessant tears,
Sinking deep into delirium –
Oh, of what use is this life!
Oh, why is fate so cruel to me!
Oh, why should only I suffer this tragedy!
Oh, even I must give up this life now!

Perpetual Motion (*Voices Unseen*)

All things begin with Death
All Death ends in Birth
Between the two is Life
Fleeting, glorious, inconsequential;
It is whatever you wish it to be.

How wilfully we ignore
The grand cycle of reality

Creation, Possibilities, Destruction
The only certainty which governs all
Visible, yet buried under the layers of lies
Which we all partake
In the name of enlightened progress
Or glorious tradition.

Old texts and tall tales
Disinterested intellectualism
Passionate activism
Angry rebellion
Passive torpor
The glittering market –
Careful and proud,
We pick our own blindfold
Merging into the herd to add our performance
To the bleating cacophony of the collective
So desperate to drown out three basic facts,
Terrifying, mind-killing.

I will not live forever,
Neither will you.
Everything I hold dear will pass,
As will yours.
Death is our final destination,
None can escape it.

No peeks are allowed behind the curtain.

Would we not go mad
If we really thought about ourselves?

2| TIPTOEING INTO A QUICKSAND

The Sutradhar Speaks

Time passed.

In the grip of sorrow,
The Old Man remained insensate –
Vital force ebbing
Like ember choking on ash.

The three chicks, now awake,
Peering curiously from the floating golden nest
Called out, guileless,
Without knowing
The meaning of life or death.

Who are you?
Why are you sad?
Who are you?
Why are you sad?
Who are you?
Why are you sad?
Who…
Why…

Something in their voices
Penetrated the wall of despair;
Blinking back his tears
The Old Man stirred,
Fading thoughts somehow refocused.

The Old Man Speaks

How I envy your innocence,
O innocent ones!
Oh what accursed creation is this
Where growing up means drinking deep
From the bitter chalice of cynical reality
Purging oneself of all that is pure
The very act of survival
A revolt against goodness.

Who is Tvashta,
Depends on who you ask and what you read.
Some called me the great *Maker*
Some, a mere *Craftsman*.
Some called me *Consciousness*
Some, the primal *Cause*.
Some called me the first *Conception*
Some, the self, *Conceived*.

I was once the engineer of possibilities
Until I faded like all things must;
Forgotten by my own creations
Discarded by my peers
Growing bitter and old,
Now in truth nothing but a witless father,
Alone in this existence
Parched for a drop of warmth
Daughter distant, son dead.

The Sutradhar Speaks

A whisper echoed across the hermitage –
Not dead. Murdered. Murdered. Murdered.

Tvashta felt a great agitation
Ripple out to him
Across the ocean of sorrow
Delivering a jolt –
Like a sudden splash of cold salt water
Brings forth painful lucidity.

Murder, Murder
Muttered the Deodar trees.
Murder, Murder
Wept the sparkling streams.
Murder, Murder
Buzzed the sacrificial flowers.
Murder, Murder
Cried the milch cows.
Murder, Murder
Screamed the broken altar.
Murder, Murder
Whispered the falling snow.

That seething cacophony of outrage
Rose to a crescendo
Then lunged back into sudden silence
And then rose again,

Pain, fear, anger, and sorrow spurting out
Inexhaustible, helpless,
From a wound freshly inflicted.

Inside their golden nest,
The three fledglings sat silent,
Without comprehension,
Full of questions.

The Sutradhar Speaks

The discord of the faceless voices
Ignited the grief of Tvashta
Into an inferno of rage
Which not even his tears could quench.

When he roared in anger
The Firmament shook,
The Sun and the Moon froze,
The lights of the world dimmed.

Ill omens appeared in the cities of men
Howling dogs chased braying donkeys –
Citizens hid in terror
The deserted streets echoed
With clattering hooves and menacing growls.

The flowers wilted.
The harvests failed.

The wails from the inner chambers,
Announced the arrival of stillborn babies.

Even the *Apsaras* collapsed in the midst of their dance
The strings of the *Gandharvas* snapped
The *Vidyadharas* crashed from the skies
The very foundations of *Svarga* began to shudder.

"Who murdered my son?"
"Who killed Trishira?"

Thus, intoned Tvashta
Again and again,
As if in a trance
While he trudged around
Demanding answers from the survivors
Scattered across the destroyed hermitage.

He first went to the Deodar,
Noblest among the trees of the hills
Its bark was charred, its leaves singed,
The branches shattered;
The *Maker* asked,
"Who murdered my son?"

"I suffered"
Said the Deodar,
"When the fury of Indra
Blazed forth, uncontrolled and irresistible."

He then went to the mountain streams,
Life veins of the Himalayas,
Once mirror-like flow now a crimson sludge
Full of stench;
The *Maker* asked,
"Who murdered my son?"

"We were polluted"
Said the mountain streams,
"When the blood-soaked Indra
Bathed in our waters."

He picked up the flowers of offering,
Scattered throughout the Hermitage
Fragrance lost, petals crushed
Trampled upon without mercy;
The *Maker* asked,
"Who murdered my son?"

"We withered"
Said the flowers,
"When we heard Indra accuse
Your son of base treachery."

He approached the milch cows,
Those kindly ones who fulfil all wishes
Piteously moo-ing, they cowered in fear

Shaking their horns;
The *Maker* asked,
"Who murdered my son?"

"Our udders became dry"
Said the cows,
"When we watched Indra and the Maruts
Ravage our hermitage in senseless rage."

He came upon the now-broken altar,
Once the holy site of the sacrifice
Its sides were kicked in,
The *dravyas* sullied;
The *Maker* asked,
"Who murdered my son?"

"I was defiled."
Said the broken altar,
"When Indra ransacked the sacrifice,
Which Trishira conducted in his name."

He looked up to the falling snow,
That pristine symbol of the celestials
Now straining against gravity
They hovered above the blood-soaked ground;
The *Maker* asked,
"Who murdered my son?"

"We will avoid"
Said the ice crystals,
"Descending upon this unhallowed earth,
Drenched with innocent Brahmin blood."

Finally, he turned to the three young birds,
Huddled against each other
Bereft of guile,
Shivering in fear;
The *Maker* asked,
"Who murdered my son?"

"Trishira was our father," said Tittiri.
"We emerged from his severed heads," said Kalapinga.
"Good bye, Grandfather," said Kapinjala.

Their innocence lost forever
The birds grew up at once, and flew away
Leaving behind the golden nest
Still warm with their scent;
The sudden ache in Tvashta's heart
Echoed with the deafening silence
Of an empty home,
Left behind by those once loved.

Unanimous though the witnesses were
The confusion of Tvashta
Knew no bounds –

How could Indra,
The King of the *Devatas*
Commit such a crime?

Tvashta Speaks

I have heard the testimony,
Yet my heart is full of questions.
Why did Trishira,
Whose weapons were truth and virtue
Become an enemy of the *Devatas*?

I will summon Agni,
The Fire which sustains creation,
Ever present and always watching;
He is the Knower of Things.

Who else is the supreme Observer
To all that happens in the three worlds?
Unbiased and incorruptible,
Who else can tell me the whole truth?

The Sutradhar Speaks

Tvashta fashioned a great altar,
In the shape of a flying falcon.
He pressed the *Soma* roots as per custom,
Straining its juices through woollen cloth.

Chanting the hymns as revealed in the *Vedas*
Tvashta offered the *Soma* juice
And invoked Agni,
That one who was the Supreme Purifier.

The air thickened.
The altar grew hot, and hotter still
Until it began to glow blue;
The ground cracked,
And as the snow turned to vapour
A pillar of fire erupted
From the centre of the altar
Announcing the arrival of radiant *Jataveda*,
The Lord of Sacrifices,
That incandescent one clad in flames.

When Tvashta beheld that Supreme form,
His agitation grew;
He addressed the fiery one
With bitter words of rebuke.

Tvashta Speaks

O all-devourer! Listen well.
My ill-fated son, when seated before you
Had poured countless oblations –
Perfectly made in form and being,

Accompanied by the proper chants,
Chanted properly;
Pure in body and spirit,
His virtue was unshakeable.

He was humble.
His speech was mild.
Free of anger, never did he utter a curse,
Though few could rival his austerities.

His benevolence extended to all.
In these icy peaks he set up this hermitage,
To engage in ceaseless *tapas*,
For the welfare of all three worlds.

Yet here he lies,
A headless cadaver,
The victim of ghastly violence,
Brazenly committed without fear.

Tell me Agni,
If the *Devatas* themselves
Succumb to the Law of the Fish,
By what right do they still claim the *Soma*?

I know you to be truthful.
For the sake of righteousness

I beg you,
Tell me how my son perished.

The Sutradhar Speaks

Come, let us rest a bit.

Please, dear reader
Look around you
While I drink some water.

No, do it, really.

The Lock (*Voices Unseen*)

Your gaze is a prison.

Doesn't really matter
Who you are
Or where you are standing,
Whether you wish it or not
Your gaze will always be a prison.

Your ego,
Lusting to conquer the world
Hijacks your brain
Whispering the urge

To map out the universe
Not as it really is,
But in human terms –
That is normal, this… strange
That is far, this… near
That is science, this… magic
That is good, this… bad
That is possible, this… impossible.

Reality bent and hammered
To fit into a you-shaped universe,
The hubris of familiarity a bunker
To avoid confronting our true insignificance
And ward off the madness and fear
Brought on by our incapability
To comprehend that which is different from us.

That is the prison of our gaze, friend.

Do you see that window?
Look outside.
Such a quaint paradox unfolds,
Which civilization tries so hard
To make us forget –
Yes, humanity might be the apex predator,
But is there any creature more fragile
Than a single lonely human?

Our cocoons alone will not sustain us,
We will not survive without each other.

<u>The Key (*The Sutradhar*)</u>

How might we coexist?
On what basis must we agree
To be bound willingly to each other,
Yet retain our very own universes?

We call them the Devatas.

Those undying ones
Are the custodians of creation
Our points of reference,
Etched on the expanse of negative space
For all egos to converge upon,
So that we can exist as discrete beings
Bound by emotions, or the lack of it
By love and hate
By duty and law and Chaos
By *Dharma*, and all that *Dharma* rejects;
Connected not only to each other
But to all of nature
Visible and invisible
And things which lie beyond the void.

That is why we worship them.

Thirty-three are they-
Twelve *Adityas*, energy of the Sun
Protectors of life,
Overseeing the cycle of seasons,
Radiant guardians of civilization;
Eleven *Rudras*, primordial power
Wild and fearsome,
Relentless in pursuit,
Fierce enforcers of cosmic balance;
Eight *Vasus*, elemental essence
Free nature spirits,
Pure and playful,
Building blocks of the universe;
Two *Ashvins*, living among us,
Riders and healers,
Curious and helpful,
Friends to the earthly realm.

<u>The Emptiness (*Voices Unseen*)</u>

No one, not even the *Devatas*
Can escape the prison of our gaze;
Distorted (by us) to human scale
Painted (by us) with mortal passions
We lose access to their awesome powers.

We think the gods have diminished
And that we have grown.

Thus do our minds unravel.

We descend down the spiral
Moving farther and farther apart
Snapping our bonds with each other
We revel in our suicidal ignorance
Hiding from reality
Choosing comfort over a truth
Too vast for our selfish ego,
As if what we cannot perceive, does not exist.

3| FORGOTTEN COVENANTS

Agni Speaks

The angry mind
Is a poisoned chalice,
An inevitable blight
Infecting any truth that it receives;
Let me go, Tvashta!

Young Trishira has passed.
Mourn him
Honour his memory
Seek the peace that waits beyond sorrow
Abandon the pursuit of vengeance
Which brings naught but pain and disquiet –
I am the witness,
I have seen.

Tvashta Speaks

What is justice,
If not the vengeance of good over evil?
Dharma is often simple –
Good is good
To be nurtured,
Evil is evil
To be crushed,
The non-violence of the weak
Cowardice,

Mercy to the unrepentant
Suicidal folly,
The silence of the graveyard
Slavery;
Though I be aeons old
Be it that my powers wane
Mistake me not for a dotard,
I am neither weak nor stupid –
My spine is still straight.

So, speak, Agni!
In front of you stands a father;
Fear not the wrath of the Immortals
Let the truth be your guide,
Conscience your comfort.
If indeed my son had erred
Praiseworthy would be the act of Indra,
But if Trishira was a blameless soul
I will deliver justice
Even unto the king of the *Devatas*.

Agni Speaks

How very human of you, Tvashta!

Since you have asked me,
And since I know the whole truth,
I shall answer.

Listen well,
I will tell you three things –
The Cause,
The Actions,
And the Event.

Yet even before that
It seems necessary
To remind you of yourself
And also perhaps
Me of myself,
So that we may rediscover
The kinship I had forgotten
The roots you had abandoned.

Long have you been a recluse, Tvashta!
Long have you shrunk,
Hiding from the world
Shunning company
You have embraced comfortable pettiness
Growing lonely and bitter –
Diminished,
Like the rest of us
Both mortal and immortal.

This gross form you now bear
Suffocating your true essence
Mirrors those who once worshipped you

Or likelier still
Those who have already forgotten you,
Just like you did yourself.

Yet this pitiful state
Is not your fate alone,
We used to be different once –
You and I and all the other celestials
Untamed and wild,
Unbound and free,
Unconstrained by human morality,
We ruled over the spectrum of possibilities
Each one of us sovereign,
A Creation unto ourselves,
All powerful,
Supreme,
Infinite,
Brahman,
Ishvara,
God.

Only the *Rishis* sensed us –
Our awesome existence was revealed
To those elevated minds,
Trained and prepared,
Forged in austerities.

They welcomed us with *Soma* juice.
Drawn by their chants

We visited their altars,
We bonded with humans
We granted them our grace-
Protection, knowledge, power
And a future;
In return they worshipped us,
Seeking to delve ever deeper
Into the unfathomable mysteries of being.

We named them *Aaryas*;
When we both honoured our sacred bond
Svarga resided on this very earth.

It was not meant to last.

Sanity is impossible for the mortal mind
When confronted by infinity
In its truest sense;
No, what they seek is the warm comfort
Of the illusion of infinity –
An illusion upholding their deepest urge
To reject limits,
Without understanding the price
Which must be paid for all power.

Foolishness.

To save the *Aaryas* from madness,
We shrunk ourselves,

To become willing prisoners of the human gaze
Functional entities
No longer infinite,
Merely many,
Merely *Devatas*,
Merely *gods*.

Yajna,
Vipaschit,
Sushanti,
Shibi,
Vibhu,
Manojav,
And in our time, *Purandara*,
The shatterer of cities;
In every cycle
The most powerful among us
The one with unshakeable will
The one who could control all his senses
The one with the power of austerities
Of more than a hundred sacrifices
Would be crowned anew,
And receive the supreme title
Indra,
The Lord of Thunder,
The King of *Devatas*,
The chief warden of the natural order.

You Tvashta, the most creative
Became our engineer;
I, Agni, the purifier
Became the incorruptible conduit
Of devotion given and earned
And witness to all that happens.

Like us
Every single celestial
Took on a role
Which the *Aaryas* could understand
And pray to;
We granted them succour and strength,
And a glimpse of the cosmic rhythm,
Even to those who were not *Rishis* –
By turning their pursuits into paths
We elevated their mundane lives
With *Sacred Purpose*,
Distilled into *Purushartha* –
The very engine of civilization.

Such was the *Way of the Aarya*
The golden age of man.

Alas, this too was not to last.

The supreme law of existence
Is that nothing lasts;

Creation, Balance, and Destruction
Follow each other without fail.

The pinnacle of Indra's reign,
From which you, Tvashta,
Had once so bitterly withdrawn
Concealed within its dazzling folds
The unceasing pull
Of the ever-spinning wheel of time.

By becoming human gods
We ourselves took on human traits,
Binding ourselves too tight
To the affairs of the world.

Submitting to *Karma* willingly
We splintered into factions –
Our very existence
Now mirroring that of our worshippers,
Became the canvas of that cosmic duality
Which humanity has named Good and Evil.

The *Way of the Aarya* began to fade and tear.

The Sutradhar Speaks

Agni spoke of many things,
While Tvashta seethed.

He spoke of all the gods
And the three Gods
The supreme Trinity who were but One;
Tvashta seethed.

He spoke of *Shakti*
The Goddess,
Who reigned beyond all understanding;
Tvashta seethed.

He spoke of the ancient rivalry
Between *Asuras* and *Devatas*
The endless civil war among celestials,
How those who worshipped the *Asuras*
Thought of the *Devatas* as Demons;
Tvashta seethed.

He spoke of the many adventures of Indra
The hymns that sprung out of them –
And Tvashta seethed and seethed
Until he could restrain himself no more.

Tvashta Speaks

Enough! Speak not to me of history,
Lament not about our origins,
Spare me the details of Indra's achievements.

It seems, Agni,
That you too have been polluted
By fear of Purandara's rage;
Why else would you delay and divert
Refusing to tell the truth
To this grieving father who stands before you?

Agni Speaks

Beware of your passions, Tvashta;
Even though you have suffered a loss
Karma doesn't need a curse
To visit those wretched souls
Incapable of controlling their senses.

This is not an idle warning,
But the start of my testimony –
This very same folly,
Triggered the chain of events
Which led to the murder of young Trishira.

Who indeed can untangle the threads of destiny?
When Sage Brihaspati,
Insulted by the King of the *Devatas*,
Left the company of celestials
It was your son who suffered an inescapable doom.

Above the mountains, beyond the skies
Nestled in the fragrant *Nandana*

Under the shadow of the *Kalpataru*
You Tvashta, had given the *Devatas* a home –
Svarga!

In that haven of bliss
The celestials roam free
In the company of worthy souls;
All desires are fulfilled
All *dukkha* is healed.

From Amaravati Indra reigns;
His consort Shachi by his side
Surrounded by the other *Devatas*
Guarded by trusty Sarama and the fierce *Maruts*,
He is the lord of mortals and immortals alike.

At the resplendent hall of thousand pillars,
Indra, wine cup in hand,
Was once immersed in merrymaking.
The heavenly *Apsaras* danced for his pleasure
To the music of *Gandharvas*.

On his golden throne he rested
Idly caressing the inlaid crystals,
When he saw his teacher arrive
Unexpected and unannounced,
Bearing a message most urgent.

The arrogant king,
Forgetting all etiquette
Remained seated;
Barely looking up,
He gestured the Sage to wait
And not interrupt the revelry.

Brihaspati Speaks

The fault is mine.

Caught up in your glory
Enjoying your prosperity
Forgetting my duties –
I failed you,
I failed your kingdom
And I failed as a teacher.

Indeed, I deserve this humiliation;
Blind to your actions,
I overlooked what you have become,
Daring not to speak
The inconvenient truths you needed to hear.

How hypocritical my anger
When I myself was oblivious
To the suffering of others

Until my own fragile ego was shattered
By that very same suffering.

I must now depart
To revive my vows,
To renew my *tapas*,
To seek the forgiveness I barely deserve
From all the three worlds.

But listen well to these words
From one who loves you still –
Your pride shackles you to the throne, Indra!
Power has gone to your head,
Just like it had to mine.

Will you look in the mirror?
Will you come back to your senses?
Will you discard your omnipotent pride?
Will you strive to burn away your dissipation
With the fire of fierce austerities?

No, you cannot.
I can see it in your face.

You still don't understand.

Know that the downfall of *Devatas* is imminent.

Agni Speaks

Thus, denouncing the King, Brihaspati,
That Knower of Secrets, smiled ruefully
Perhaps on fate, perhaps on himself;
Turning his back to the world of the celestials
That supreme sage departed.

Shachi began to weep.
The music stopped.
The dancers froze.
The wine turned bitter.
Sarama howled in anguish.

A whispering wind arrived
Unbidden, cold;
The petals of dead *Parijaat* flowers
Caressed the feet of the shell-shocked *Devatas*
Reminding them of long-forgotten death.

Indra leapt up from his throne,
Swaying wildly,
His drunken haze fading fast.
He flung away his goblet
And ran after the preceptor.

But not even an Immortal
Can escape the weave

Of Time and *Karma*.
Brihaspati was gone;
It was too late to make amends.

Standing alone at the gates of Amaravati,
A cold chill went down Shakra's spine.

4| CHAINS OF FATE

Agni Speaks

To the Grandfather's abode the *Devatas* rushed.
In Brahmaloka, that heaven of serene bliss,
Where time itself grew imperceptible
They bowed before the Creator
Shedding copious tears
Like naughty children most repentant.

Indra Speaks

O Prajapati!
You are our only refuge.
The radiant Brihaspati, our preceptor,
Insulted by our actions,
Abandoned us
Like Shri abandons an *Adharmic* abode.

Tell us where that supreme sage is,
So that we may beg his forgiveness,
Then with all due honours bring him back
To restore the lustre of our desolate *Svarga*.

Brahma Speaks

Two things are inevitable.
The passage of Time,
The fruits of *Karma*.

Like water released from a broken dam,
Brihaspati has left you *Devatas*.
One day he will return;
But until that time arrives
A new priest you must seek.

Indra Speaks

O God! O Almighty! O Prajapati!
Who is that exalted one,
Worthy enough to be our guide?
Who in the three worlds,
Can shoulder that immense responsibility?

Without a teacher,
Dharma abandons the society,
Strength abandons the strong,
Hope abandons the weak,
Intent abandons the student,
Directions abandon the traveller,
Energy abandons the farmer,
Saraswati abandons the scholar,
Lakshmi abandons the householder,
Restraint abandons the ruler,
Valour abandons the soldier,
Fame abandons the king –
Verily, life itself abandons the body.

Shame on me.
Shame on my conduct.
Cursed be my pride
Which led the son of Angirasa to abandon the *Devatas*.
Without his counsel,
We celestials are like a rudderless boat,
Tossed around by the whims of fate
Precarious, uncertain,
Poised on the edge of catastrophe.

Agni Speaks

When the Grandfather heard
Indra's contrite words,
He was amused.

He knew the past, present, and future,
And the truth which lay hidden in the king's heart.
Then that shaper of destiny,
The one born from the navel,
Instructed Purandara –
"Go seek out young Trishira,
Son of Tvashta the Maker.
Take refuge in his austerities,
Make him your priest,
Conduct immense sacrifices
For the welfare of the three worlds."

Dark became Indra's face
When Lord Brahma mentioned you
And your learned son.

Indra Speaks

How could that upstart *Dasa*,
A half-*Asura* no less,
Become the priest of the *Devatas*?

I had rebuked his father
Tvashta the *Maker*;
In his lust for power
He married the *Asura* princess
And gave his daughter to the Sun.

Pleading his innocence,
That jealous Tvashta became a recluse;
Banished from *Svarga* by me,
He abandoned his wife
And now roams the three worlds
Alone and without happiness.

How can that vagrant Tvashta's son be my priest?
Will he too not grow jealous,
Will he too not desire my throne?

Afraid of *Vishvarupa's* penance
I had once sent the *Apsaras*

To break his vows;
Will he not remember?
Will he not seek revenge?

O Grandfather!
There must be someone else
Of nobler birth,
And more gracious disposition,
Who can become our priest.

Brahma Speaks

O king of the *Devatas*, heed my advice –
Only fools obsess over birth and lineage,
Only fools value gilded words over knowledge;
The wise are able to sift the chaff from the wheat.

Trishira the three-headed ascetic,
Is established in *Dharma*.
Steadfast in his vows,
His severe penance had lasted for a thousand years.

The apsaras you sent then, O Indra,
Failed in their task.
When Trishira rejected those beautiful ones,
Defying their sultry and wide-hipped charms,
His energy increased manifold.

High upon the mountains
That innocent sage
Blazing with the fruits of his *tapas*
Is tirelessly engaged in difficult rituals
For the happiness of all three worlds.

Go to that exalted *Vishvarupa*
Propitiate him with all the honours due
Appoint him as your priest
Learn from him the three virtues
Compassion, selflessness, and love;
Start a new age.

Agni Speaks

Heeding the words of Druhinah,
Purandara bade him farewell,
With a heart heavy with reluctance.
In the company of the celestials,
He travelled to the snow-swept north,
In search of the Himalayan hermitage,
Of Tvashta's radiant son.

A beautiful haven of peace
Was the abode of the son of Tvashta.

Beasts, birds, trees, and insects
Breathed the same clean air,
Lived together sans rancour,

All of them serving the kindly one
Who had conquered all desire.

His hair darker than the moonless night
His skin covered in cremation ashes
His life force radiant with fearsome austerities,
Shining like hope amongst jagged, icy peaks,
Tendrils of vapour swirled about his body
Like wild vines entwining the *Ashwatha* tree –
Trishira was a pure white flame.

O Tvashta, he was like a second Sun
Floating above an ocean of molten snow.

His three heads were pleasant to look at
One drenched by a never-ending stream of *Soma*,
The other observing this world
Filled with *Maya*, intoxicating like wine.
His third head chanted the *Vedas* –
The perfect Word rumbled across the valleys
Sonorous and deep,
Like rolling thunder,
Bringing delight to the divine and the mortal alike.

The *Devatas* descended on this hermitage
Like a meteor shower in the House of *Mithuna*.

Your innocent son welcomed them.

PART THREE

MAHAPAAP

The Sutradhar wears the mask of *a runaway kite*.

1| THE IRRESISTIBLE

The odd couple (*The Sutradhar*)

One day, I saw a man fighting his mind!

The man said, O Mind!
Why do you not listen to me?
Why do you not learn?
Why do you insist
On getting hurt, again and again?
O Mind! Why do you love pain?

The mind answered, O Man!
What worth is freedom
That doesn't allow you pain?
How will you cross the river,
If you don't let go of the bank?
O Man! Why are you so afraid?

The man said, O Mind!
That world out there
Is not a nice place.
There is you, and there are others.
Why do you not understand this?
O Mind! Why do you remain innocent?

The mind answered, O Man!
Even if you don't want to be,

You are a part of this world.
Look outside – is not the world a mirror,
Reflecting only what you make of it?
O Man! Why are you so selfish?

The man said, O Mind!
Beware of smiling faces,
What they call love is a lie.
Why do you keep trusting,
When trust is always broken?
O Mind! Why do you not learn?

The mind answered, O Man!
Lighten your heart,
Let go of this wretched bitterness –
Extend your hands between the bars,
Reach out beyond your self-made cage.
O Man! Why are you so cynical?

I sold the man one story,
I hummed a lullaby for free;
Then I walked away
Not looking back –
The man slept
The mind dreamt
For a little while they did not fight,
Perhaps this is what they call life!

Trishira Speaks

Tell me, O noble Indra,
Tell me O Mitra, O Varuna, and O Vayu,
Tell me O *Maruts*, O *Vidyadharas*, and O *Gandharvas*,
What brings you all to my remote idyll?

Indra Speaks

O wise one,
The *Devatas* are like cattle
Lost in the thorny maze of the forest of fate.
Abandoned by sage Brihaspati,
We possess neither a teacher nor a protector.

O sage, on the advice of Lord Brahma,
I request you to become our priest.
Conduct for us a great *Yajna*
Share out the oblations as per *Dharma*.
May our strength increase.
May our weapons grow more fearsome.
Harnessing the power of the *Soma*,
May the *Devatas* become mighty in war.

Agni Speaks

When Trishira heard the words of Indra,
His heart was filled with great disquiet.

Trishira Speaks

Accept my apologies.
I am too young,
Without any experience,
lacking in wisdom.
How can this unworthy one
Be the successor of mighty Brihaspati?
Content in my present state,
Without any ambition,
I wish to carry on my austerities
For the benefit of all three worlds.

Therefore, O Indra,
Forgive me!
Find a different one to be your priest.
Establish him with honour.
Let him conduct the *Yajna*
To satisfy all that you desire.

Agni Speaks

Indra loomed over Trishira,
Scowling, threatening –
His fury ignited,
Unused to being denied.

Indra Speaks

You dare to refuse Lord Brahma then?
How can you serve the world,
When you refuse to serve the *Devatas*?
What use is your learning?
What use are your austerities?
O Trishira! Why do you forget
The responsibility that follows knowledge?
Why do you hide in these lonely places?
Why do you shun society
Like your father, Tvashta, grace-robbed?

So, I ask you once more –
Attend my court.
Become my priest.
Be radiant with success.

The end of the tunnel (*The Sutradhar*)

At the cusp of every turn
At every new beginning
The mirage of peace appears,
A shimmering hope
To innocent minds.

Then again
Being immortal is no escape from the fear

Secreted by every heart
Poisoning the oasis
Shaming those who hope
To leave us languishing,
Bent over the crutch cynical –
It is the way of the world
That reality overwhelms good intentions.

O Mother!
Why is the world like this?
Why are we so weak?
Why do you test us so?

Agni Speaks

Unable to deny Indra,
Trishira,
Heart heavy with dire foreboding
Agreed to Indra's demands
And performed a great *Yajna*.

In this very hermitage
The *arani* were rubbed
The fire was lit
The *Soma* was pressed and strained
The *Vedas* were chanted.

Amidst the cheers of the *Devatas*,
The sacred flame leapt forth

From the centre of the altar.
The *Soma* Juice
Heated, cooled, offered, and received,
Was shared among the *Devatas*,
Each one accepting what was due;
The power of the ritual
Amplified by the energy of Trishira
Manifested within the *Devatas* as intense heat.

Bolstered by that *Yajna*
All the *Devatas* set out to do battle.
Intolerant and mighty
Those *Soma* drinkers raided
the *Daitya* cities,
Shattering their very foundations.

Tormented by the *Devatas*
The *Asuras* were scattered in all directions,
Like untended husks of wheat
Caught in a fierce norwester.

In that hour of crisis for the *Asura* race
When destruction looked all but certain,
The defeated *Asuras*,
Drained of spirit
Overcome by misery
Converged on the green-crested hermitage
Of great-souled Shukra,
Their revered teacher.

Led by their King Virochan,
In one voice they pleaded
To that radiant one,
Once part of Shambhu,
For wisdom and guidance.

King Virochan Speaks

O *Asuracharya*!
You know me as the son of Emperor Prahlada,
The greatest of our race –
That virtuous one
Whom Vishnu Himself saved
When He erupted from the pillar
In His terrifying lion form.

Seeking to extend my ancestor's glory,
Forever have I acted per *Dharma*
Protecting the weak,
Punishing the evil,
Sustaining the good.

Yet doom is upon us today.
In the face of Indra's onslaught
Our valour has failed,
Our weapons have become sterile,
Countless have died,
Many more have lost their all.

O Teacher! We seek refuge in your knowledge.
Tell us how we may repulse the mighty *Devatas*
Salvage our lineage and prosperity,
And regain our honour.

Agni Speaks

Desiring to protect those who sought protection
Shukra, the wise son of Bhrigu
Invoked the power of his austerities;
An invincible aegis,
Golden-hued,
Shining like the sun,
Crackling with power,
Shrouded the hermitage –
Like a womb shields the baby within.

Then wise Shukracharya
Gave counsel to King Virochan.

Shukracharya Speaks

You have not become weak, O King!
The *Devatas* are drunk with *Soma*
Empowered by the *Yajna* of Trishira;
That *Hotar* is the son of Tvashta,
The estranged husband to your sibling Virochana.

Send her as your messenger to the Himalayas.
Let your sister remind your nephew
Of his blood ties to the *Asura* nation.
Let that auspicious one tell her son
Of the plight of his relatives and clanspeople.

Agni Speaks

Thus counselled,
The *Asura* king summoned his twin,
The lotus-eyed Virochana
Austere and pious
Engaged in a vow of silence
Ever since her separation from Tvashta.

King Virochan Speaks

Make haste, beloved sister,
The *Devatas* have discovered this haven.
Can you not hear shrieking *Maruts*
Riding the roaring winds?
Can you not feel the trembling earth
Shake with every step of Airavata?
Sarama has sniffed us out –
Following her, our mortal enemies approach.

Find your energetic son,
Tell him of the danger confronting his kinsmen.

Convince him to lend us his strength,
So that our race may survive
This barbaric assault of the immortal ones.

2| THE IMMOVABLE

Agni Speaks

On the command of her brother, the king,
Virochana, wise in the arts of *Maya*, took flight.
She sped like a beautiful meteor
Streaking gold across the azure skies of *Jambudvipa*
Towards those snow-capped peaks that housed her son
Even as the *Devatas* descended upon Shukra's abode.

The Asuras prepared their last stand.

Chanting the name of *Shiva*,
They shared among themselves
Hopeless courage,
Such that even those who were cowering in fear
Found peace in their minds
By the grace of the Lord of Kailasa.

The sound of their singing enraged the *Devatas;*
Those intolerant ones
Furiously assaulted Shukra's *Yogic* shield
Whilst the *Asuras* sang ever louder.

Lord of Kailasa, we seek refuge in you
Purest One, we seek refuge in you
O Nataraja, we seek refuge in you
Supreme Innocence, we seek refuge in you
Master of Knowledge, we seek refuge in you

A rumbling resonance swept the land.
The weapons of the *Devatas* echoed in shock
When they were repulsed by Shukra's power.
Yet again and again the *Devatas* charged,
Untiring, their vigour augmented by *Soma* –
Until even the strength of Shukra began to fade
Along with the aegis that cocooned his home.

Husband of Shakti, we seek refuge in you
Vanquisher of Tripura, we seek refuge in you
Drinker of Poison, we seek refuge in you
Destroyer of Manmatha, we seek refuge in you
Bearer of Ganga, we seek refuge in you

Sensing the annihilation of their enemy
The *Devatas* battered that weakening barrier
While the *Asuras* sang on
Casting away all regrets
Prepared, one and all,
For a final battle to death.

Self Born, we seek refuge in you
Boon Giver, we seek refuge in you
Skull Wearer, we seek refuge in you
Trident Holder, we seek refuge in you
Ashen One, we seek refuge in you

A great sorrow then arose.
Like a tidal wave resonating with defiant faith

It swept through the world
Bearing the voices of besieged *Asuras,*
They who had surrendered to the Supreme *Yogi*
That refuge beyond all fear and hope.

God of gods, we seek refuge in you
Lord of Time, we seek refuge in you
Eternal Truth, we seek refuge in you
Remover of Sins, we seek refuge in you
Master of Universe, we seek refuge in you

The heart of Trishira was filled with sudden disquiet.
His tongue refused to pronounce the *Mantras*
The ladle of offerings slipped from his hand;
When he looked up,
He saw his mother descend from the sky
Her face drenched in tears.

Virochana Speaks

Cursed be my womb,
That my own blood became the cause
For the demise of my people.
Oh son, because of your deeds
The world would know me
As the mother of a traitor.
Did your mind not revolt even once,
Before you committed this treason to your kin?

Agni Speaks

Trishira fell to his mother's feet
Unable to comprehend
The anger in her gentle voice.

Trishira Speaks

What is my sin, O Mother,
That you denounce me thus
With sword-like words,
Which stab my heart?

Do you not know
That this son of yours
Alone in this remote hermitage
Perseveres with his penance
Day and night
Unperturbed by snowstorms
Unaffected by biting winds
Through hunger, pain, and fatigue
Thinking of naught
But the happiness of truth
And the attainment of *moksha* for all three worlds?

Virochana Speaks

Alas, my son! What use is your penance,

When it enables a merciless slaughter of innocents?
What else is treachery,
If not your service to our hated enemy?
What *moksha* is there,
For the *Asuras* killed by the violent Indra?

At this very moment,
Even as we speak,
The king of the *Devatas,*
Emboldened by your *Yajna*,
Assaults the final refuge of your tribe.

Both the *Devatas* and the *Daityas*,
Exist to balance this chaotic creation
Which is in truth the veil of *Maya*
Beyond which lies the One,
Formless yet of infinite forms –
Hiranyagarbha,
The cosmic Source whom the seekers seek.

What is this Creation,
But the playground of that Supreme Truth?
A confounding test for us to answer
Throughout our life,
Across many lives?

Grasping at the thread of liberation
With all the power of our *Purushartha*

We learn to pay our debts and trim our fat
Until we reach the perfect Zero –
Only then do our eyes open
To see the path revealed
Shimmering through the great expanse,
Lying beyond the senses,
Leading us to that One destination,
Incomprehensible yet inevitable.

By your deeds, Trishira,
You upset the Order of Creation –
Know that the universe abhors absolutes
Choosing instead to exist in flux
Dancing on the threads of sublime, chaotic balance.

The one who eats is also food.
The one who rules is also ruled.
Beauty fades with the lines of age.
The night promises the dawn to come.
Certainty does not exist.
Everything changes.

We are the rule breakers.
We are the boon seekers.
We are the risk-takers.
We are the mistaken ones,
The mortal enemies
Of meekly knowing our place.

Is it not us *Asuras*
Who are the changebringers
From the oppressive inertia
Which shackles the world of *Devatas*?

A world without the *Asuras*
Will be a world of diseased rust
Stuck in one place;
The very law of *Karma* would cease to work,
The path to *Moksha* lost forever.
Unable to dissipate their unbearable energy,
The helpless *Devatas* would despair –
Burning down the world before its time.

O Son of Tvashta!
Listen to your mother,
Recognize the call of your *Daitya* blood,
Understand the will of *Dharma*,
Do not let the cosmic balance be destroyed.

My son! Rescue us from annihilation.

Agni Speaks

Rebuked by his mother
Trishira stopped the *Yajna;*
Starved of oblations,
The fire grew weak.

Trishira Speaks

I have been subjected
To a betrayal most vile;
Never did I imagine
That Indra would choose war
To waste the power of my austerities.

Yet the pain I feel
Is nothing compared to the sorrow
Of those whose lives were ruined
By the wanton destruction
Wrought by the power-mad Indra.

I will not run away.

I am not a coward.
I am the son of Tvashta,
The grandson of Prahlada;
In my veins run the blood
Of both Diti and Aditi.

I will not run away.

Tell me Mother,
What is your wish now?
How can I help
Those still endangered
By the rampaging *Devatas?*

Virochana Speaks

O son! By the power of your *Yajna*
The *Devatas* grew strong;
Grant the *Asuras* that very same strength
So that they may defend their honour
And repulse their enemies.

Trishira Speaks

I will agree to do this,
Even though I know
That violence only feeds the cycle of war.

This burden is mine.

It was I who did not have the courage
To say no to the demands of Indra.
It was I who did not have the foresight
To understand the will of the *Devatas*.
It was I who had forgotten
The heritage I received from you.

A moment will come, perhaps,
When I would gain the right
To seek forgiveness for my errors,
But now is the time to act.

Let me pour what remains of my strength
Into this very same *Yajna*
And let the sacred fire pass it on to my relatives
So that they may be spared annihilation.

Agni Speaks

Then Trishira, picking up a fistful of dust
From his mother's feet
Chanted the supreme *Mantra*
And threw it into the fire pit.

Fuelled by his austerities,
Heated by his anger,
A single spark rose from the altar
And began to grow,
Until it shone like a second sun.

Far away, at Shukra's abode
The *Devatas* faltered.
An unknown dread filled their heart
Draining their limbs of all strength;
Overcome by weakness and confusion
The *Devatas* lost the will to fight,
Their weapons slipping out from their grips,
And clattering to the ground.

The *Asuras* felt a surge of power.
Hope returned to their hearts;
Led by the fey spectre of King Virochan,
The *Daityas* rushed out of the hermitage,
With war cries that shook the earth
The scattered the *Devatas* in front of them.

In terror, the sons of Aditi fled
Covering the ten directions with dust
The victorious *Asuras* returned to their cities,
Songs on their lips and tears in their eyes
Lamenting the deaths of friends and kin.

Mournful and cold,
An unnatural night descended upon the earth
While the spark slowly collapsed in front of Trishira.

The battle was over.

3| THE INEVITABLE

The Balance Sheet (*Voices Unseen*)

There is a price to pay.

Under the Law
Whether you know it or not
Even for one single breath
There is always a price.

Neither can you haggle
Nor can you bribe
Karma gives no discounts
There is always a price.

The longer you flee
The higher your dues
Even death is no end
Always, there is a price to pay.

Mostly you give
Sometimes you receive
Yet never are you free
There is always a price.

Trapped in the cycle
Your birth is a debt
Virtue or vice
There is always a price.

You cannot escape
Until you know the truth,
This world is a lie
And you are the joke
But no one is laughing
For they all are you
Wearing a mask
Like you they are confused;
Stuck in the grind
Slave to their craves
For good or for bad
Bound by the price,
In black or in red
Dragged by the chains
Birth after birth
Death after death,
You cannot escape
You cannot escape
There is always a price to pay.

The Sutradhar Speaks

In the starlit silence
Tvashta wept;
Agni watched him
Flickering,
Impassive,
Lost in his own
thoughts.

The world wept with Tvashta.

The Deodar trees wept
Red sap streaking its barks
The mountain stream wept
Sadness frothing over its banks
The flowers wept
Dewdrops freezing in the cold
The cows wept
Salting their milk with tears
The altar wept
Vermillion and ghee glistening on its steps
The snowflakes wept too
Finally melting in sorrow.

Tvashta Speaks

The cobwebs clear.

My time has passed,
And all I am left with are regrets;
For the words not spoken
For the days spent apart
For all the little arguments
Those times I didn't smile –
I am sorry, son.

Across the three worlds
The sadness of your passing

Clutched at my heart;
I arrived here faster than a streak of thought
Yet it is too late now
To tell you how proud I am,
To tell you what a great son you were.
It is too late
I know,
I know,
For me to say sorry,
For me to have regrets;
Yet here I am
Sorry, full of regret –
What else can a father do?

Yes, it is too late,
And I am here
Left behind,
Alone;
My time has passed.

Finish your story, O Agni
Tell me how my son was killed.

Agni Speaks

I shall speak.
I was the witness.

Burning with shame
Maddened with rage
The Lord of the *Devatas*
Rushed towards this hermitage.

The clouds laid a dark siege
The thunder battered his humble hut
The rain fell –
Sharp, like pins coated with poison
The winds raged incessant
Scraping, attacking,
Malice palpable
To all under Trishira's protection.

Kind young Trishira hugged the trees;
With his soft voice, he comforted the cows
With his golden body, he shielded the streams
With his nimble hands, he tended the altar –
Then, calming his vast mind,
He waited.

The ground shook when Indra landed.
All life shrank back in terror
As if this beautiful hermitage
Had all of a sudden
Plunged into *Yama's* domain of death;
Only Purandara and the three-headed sage

Stood facing each other
Within that black-and-white tear in reality.

With his voice full of anger,
Indra addressed Trishira with cruel words
Pouring out the contempt and fear
Which lay in his heart.

Indra Speaks

O traitor! O worst of sages!
Never in the history of this age
Or the countless ones preceding this
Has the world witnessed such faithlessness
As shown by you today.

At the cusp of our victory
You stabbed us in the back
Snatching away from the *Devatas*
The golden chance
To rid the world of the *Asuras*
Once and for all.

Even if you are a sage
Even if you know the *Brahman*
Even if you are protected by *Dharma*
Know that there will be no escape
From my punishment for your betrayal.

Trishira Speaks

Your hollow words
Confirm to me once again
Just how far, O King,
You have fallen.

Ruled by fear,
A slave to your senses,
Unworthy of your name
You have long abandoned the path of *Dharma*.

O weak one!
If you want to fight the *Asuras*,
Become strong!
Perform penance!
Increase your *tapas*!
Why did you misuse the strength of my *Yajna*
Meant to bring welfare to the entire universe?
Why did you bring shame to my name
Tainting my penance
With your relentless thirst for war?

Understand this, O proud one,
It is your own lack of power
Your own lack of foresight,
Your own lack of wisdom
That has led you to this catastrophe;

There can be no scapegoat but you,
There is no one else to blame.

Yet I cannot escape my share
My very own burden of responsibility
For this wanton destruction
Wrought by your reckless lust.

No longer will I be your priest
But will start my penance anew
To cleanse my soul
From your touch of evil.

Agni! Be my witness!
Shankara! I surrender unto you!

Agni Speaks

Answering his call
I emerged from this altar,
To bear witness –
The great yogi Trishira,
Immersed in meditation
Surrounded by countless *Bhutas*
Who served The Lord of Kailasa.

I saw the tears in his eyes
Even though his senses
Had already withdrawn from the world.
O Tvashta, I saw his body,

Bathed in ethereal golden light,
Grow ever more vast
As if it would cover the entire firmament
Just like *Hari* did
When He took the three steps
To subdue the great Asura, Bali.

Then I witnessed Indra,
Fear masking his face,
Creep up behind Trishira
And summoning his thunderbolt,
Strike down your son.

The innocence of the world shattered when your son fell.

"*Shame Shame*", cried the *Bhutas* of *Shankara.*
"*Shame Shame*", cried the mountains.
"*Shame Shame*", cried the ten directions.
"*Shame Shame*", cried the boundless heavens.

A golden soul
Blinding,
Radiant,
Emerged from the body of your son;
Slowly it rose above the hermitage,
Bathed in a fragrant shower of petals made of light.
The seven celestial sages appeared in the sky
To show him the path
Towards the deathless realms among the stars.

Yet Indra was not satisfied.
With his shameful deed done,
Indra ordered a poor woodcutter
To decapitate the corpse of your son.
Quaking with fear
The woodcutter refused time and again,
But finally had to submit
To the many threats and promises of Indra.

His hands shaking,
The woodcutter began his gruesome task.
For every head he chopped,
A tiny bird emerged from your son's body.

When he was done,
The shivering woodcutter,
Drenched in the spurting fountains of blood,
Finally noticed the fledglings.
Unable to withstand
The innocent gaze of the newborn three
He ran;
Throwing away his axe,
He jumped into a canyon
Never to be seen again.

Even after that gruesome carnage,
The King of the Devatas was not satisfied.
Indra summoned his *Maruts*;

Roaring with laughter
They rampaged around the hermitage
Destroying everything in sight.

Then a pitch-black hag
Rose up from the Earth;
Her hair was matted
Her eyes were red
Her teeth was white
Blood dripped from her tongue
Her skeletal hands were long
The skulls on her skirt were laughing.

She seized the lightning of Indra
She drove away the terrified *Maruts;*
With hideous shrieks
That terrible being chased Purandara
Seeking vengeance for *Brahmahatya* –
The cold-blooded murder of a Brahmin.

In terror, Indra fled.

Within the empty hermitage
Those three helpless birds
Wept.

My testimony ends here, Tvashta.

PART FOUR

RAGEBORN

The Sutradhar wears the mask of *Raga Malkauns*.

1| AN INSTRUMENT OF JUSTICE

The Sutradhar Speaks

Silently the snow fell.

Agni flickered for a while,
Then left.

Silently the snow fell.

Sorrow and anger
Congealed around Tvashta,
Thick and heavy,
Suffocating,
Yet death was not the release
The old man sought.

Silently the snow fell.

He did not stir
When Virochana arrived,
Hair undone
Her face streaked with tears;
He stood and watched
As she wildly beat her chest,
And shedding copious tears
Cursed Indra and the *Devatas*.

Silently the snow fell.

In silence,
They cremated their son.
In silence,
They watched the black smoke
Spiral up from the pyre.
In that silence,
They heard the emptiness
Raging in their breasts.

Silently the snow fell.

Night turned to day
Day turned to night
Again and again.

Benumbed and hollow,
Tvashta and Virochana
Stood watching the ashes
Beside the pyre long gone cold,
Silent,
Legs frozen to the ground
Their fingers grasping each other.

Like rocks in a river
They withered together in that silence,
Their sadness slowly taking shape
As the currents of time
Passed them by.

In silence they watched the snow fall.

When Indra leapt into the abyss of *Adharma*
The *Devatas* lost the strength
To fulfil their tasks.

Chaos spread;
The order of the universe
Unravelled, bit by bit.

Cracks appeared in the three worlds,
Injustice prospered
Heat and warmth abandoned the Sun
Pollution obscured the stars
Night and day melded;
Ushas, the supreme dawn
That joy of all life
Was nowhere to be found
While the *Devatas*
Powerless to stop the collapse
Huddled in *Svarga*,
Terrified by visions
Of the lady of retribution.

Silently the snow fell.

The rage of Tvashta
The grief of Virochana

The empty hermitage of Trishira
Became the centre
Of a swirling vortex of emotions –
Discontent, Anger, Sorrow
Pouring out in response
To the pall of oppression
Which covered the fallen worlds.

Still, the snow fell, in silence.

Then Tvashta lit the altar.
Then Tvashta pressed the *Soma*.
Then Tvashta whispered the *Mantra*.

Like a woman giving birth,
The mountains convulsed –
Magma seeped out from the deepest ruptures;
The fallen snow sizzled
Turning into steam
Then mating with ash
To form a thick black fog.

A great being emerged from the shadows.

The Rageborn.
The Restrainer.
The Obstacle.

Ahi,
The Serpent.

Vritra,
The Dragon.

Vritra Speaks

I am born, father.

Tvashta Speaks

Go forth, and avenge your brother.
Go forth, and destroy Indra.

2| THE FOOTSTEPS OF PANDEMONIUM

The Sutradhar Speaks

I know what you are thinking.

Why should I care?
Let the powerful fight each other
Let them be destroyed;
Why should I care?

There is no Indra in my life,
I can see no Agni
No Mitra-Varuna
Nor Brahma, Vishnu and Maheshvara
Neither do I see the terrible *Asuras*.
The *Daityas* and *Danavas* have not oppressed me
The *Rakshasas* have left me alone
The *Devatas* were not to be found
When I needed help.

Why should I bother?

You have all these questions,
And I have none of the answers;
I only have this story.

Bear with me, please.
Forget, for a moment,
All the labels –

Heroes and villains
Good and evil
Divine and mortal,
Instead, let us embrace
At least for a little bit,
The weak ones who fall
The flawed ones who transgress
Tarnished gold and chipped bowls
The sinking vessel,
Let us embrace all that is broken.

Let us help each other muster courage
To face the fundamental truth –
All of us are imperfect.

Yet, is it my fate to just be
The sum of my imperfections,
Or can I dare to hope,
That one day I too can become
A song complete and bountiful
Composed in the joy of painful *tapas*?

Beyond the grind of harsh reality,
Beyond the all-pervasive cynicism taught by life,
Is it just a fool's hope that hope exists,
That on our very birth we have not been
Checkmated by circumstances?

Am I stupid to believe that through struggle
We can break through the barrier of futility,
To touch something greater than ourselves,
Once,
Just once,
At least, just once –
So that for one single fleeting moment
We may see the blinding flash of Truth,
Darshan,
And thus become free?

But tell me,
If this hope is not there,
What else is left?

No.
This fool says-
The land can be purified with blood,
Destroyed temples can be rebuilt with sweat,
A broken *murti* can be healed with grace,
The lost can return home,
If their hearts hear our call.

What else is life,
But believing in earnest
That redemption is real,
That it is worth carrying on?

Come, let us abandon all judgements,
And journey along the threads of *Karma*.

Unleashed by the fury of Tvashta,
Vritra began his rampage.

Like a shuddering avalanche
Ahi emerged from the hermitage of Trishira
And took flight –
Roaring again and again,
He flew over the skies of the continents,
His great shadow blocked the sun
Drawing out the ones who dwelt in darkness.

Murderers.
Rapists.
Thieves.
Liars and oathbreakers,
Prophets of falsehood,
Sellers of venom,
The jealous ones,
And the destroyers of nations –
They all worshipped the Serpent,
Drinking from that inexhaustible well of malice
To grow ever more in power.

Kaleyas.
That is what they called themselves,
The followers of Vritra.

Not all who look like men are humans.

The loathsome *Kaleyas* shackled *Jambudvipa,*
Chaining her with ninety-nine citadels of power;
From those unhallowed depths they streamed out
Seething with hatred against the cosmic balance –
Some in the open,
Some in disguise,
Yet others remaining invisible.

Under the great wings of Vritra,
The *Kaleyas* began their war upon the three worlds,
Spreading their corruption,
Infecting humanity,
Tainting all life.

Black storms followed the flight of Ahi
Tidal waves smashed into mountain tops
Unable to withstand his anger
Bhudevi split into bottomless ravines
Sucking in innocents
To the netherworlds of *Rasatala.*

Poisonous fumes rose from the abandoned dead
Merging with Ahi's venom into a toxic miasma
That pitiless fog spread across the land and the sea;
Birds fell dead in their flight
Fishes drowned in acid.

Sarama, the brave messenger of Indra,
Blocked the path of the gigantic Ahi.
That divine hound,
The doom of the *Panis*,
Spoke words of conciliation.

Sarama Speaks

Who are you, O slithering one?
Why do you advance against *Svarga*?
What is your grudge against the *Devatas?*
If you desire peace,
Tell us, by what means will you be pacified?
If it is war you seek,
Know that the power of the immortals,
Led by the valiant Indra,
Is infinite.
Therefore stop this foolishness.
Submit to Indra,
Come under his protection;
Let peace reign once more in the world.

The Sutradhar Speaks

Vengeance.
Destruction.
Anger.
So much anger.

How dare he!
How dare Indra talk of peace!
How dare the *Devatas* threaten him!

The Great Serpent,
In his final moment of clarity
Just before surrendering to Chaos,
Remembered his father's command for one last time.

'Go forth, and avenge your brother.
Go forth, and destroy Indra.'

Vritra roared once more.
There was no place his voice did not reach.
Forgetting all her responsibilities,
Sarama fled in terror.

The world understood
That there would be no mercy.

When Ahi looked up,
His many coloured eyes flashed
As if sunlight on mercury;
He saw *Svarga* looming above the earth,
And his wrath ignited the air around his body.

Like a flaming meteor,
He streaked up, towards Amaravati

Where the *Devatas* huddled in terror-
Their wisdom lost,
Unable to comprehend the unfolding calamity.

Drained of all powers
By their surrender to *Adharma*,
The immortal ones felt the noose of *Karma*
Tighten around their necks.

3| CATACLYSM

The Sutradhar Speaks

At the centre of *Jambudvipa*
Stands a golden mountain no mortal can climb.

The immensely tall Meru
Is the axis of all three worlds;
The Meru cannot be found
The Meru cannot be reached
The Meru cannot be seen –
The five peaks of Meru only reveal themselves
To those it deems worthy,
To those who have walked the Path,
To those who have followed the Way.

To reach *Svarga*,
The residence of the immortals,
One has to achieve the impossible –
Climb the mighty Meru,
All eighty-four thousand *yojanas* of it
Literally breaking free past the confines of this earth.

Yet this impossibility was precisely the point
Of a task designed deliberately,
To underscore the limits of mortal power
Inspiring hope among the faithful,
And despair for the disobedient.

Yet what is an impossibility
In a world where a Vritra has been born?

Vritra is not bound by rules;
No, the Great Serpent is the destroyer of Order.
Ahi can find what cannot be found,
Ahi can reach what cannot be reached,
Ahi can see what cannot be seen;
No foe can escape
The fiery gaze of Vishvarupa's brother.

The Great Serpent howled in rage
At the home of his enemies
And all that it stood for.

Under the pitch-black sky,
The air became still.
The sea held its breath,
As if a silent mirror.
No whispers were heard in the forest deep
No splashes in the river from the jumping fish
The trees forbade their leaves to rustle
Empty were the veins of concrete jungles;
All those who breathed held their breath,
Cowering,
Waiting,
Scarcely understanding,
Why an unknown dread had suddenly paralysed their hearts.

From the foot of Mount Meru
Vritra began to rise,
Spiralling around the four faces of the mountain
Made of Gold, Rubies, Crystals and Lapis Lazuli.

Furious was his ascent,
Relentless was his drive,
Like a tornado gathering power
The Great Serpent soared towards *Svarga*
Leaving chaos and destruction in his wake.

The journey of Vritra through the foothills
Uprooted trees and scorched the streams
Ravaging the teeming forests adorned with gems.
Shrieking in terror the birds and the animals fled;
But Ahi did not care,
He kept flying higher.

In the valleys and the groves of Meru
Countless ascetics practised the austerities;
Their hermitages were swept away,
Their sacred fires were doused
Ignoring their feeble curses,
Ahi soared upwards.

The realm of shadows lie above the forests
Home of the *Pitri,* glorious ancestors;
Carried to Meru by the cremation smoke,
Subsisting on the offerings of their descendants,

Those hungry ones wait in silence,
For release at the end of the cycle.

All are born in debt to the *Pitris;*
Without them there would be no us,
Yet how conveniently they are judged
How easily they are forgotten
As if we too will not join them
At that very same destination.

Vritra the rageborn had no debt.
Immune to the power of the *Pitris*,
Like a storm he passed through the gloom;
The spirits scattered in confusion
Falling down to earth
To become the devourers of uncontrolled emotions.

Rising from the realm of shadows
Ahi assaulted the sunlit lower peaks
Glorious, beautiful, the haven of desire,
Home to the minor celestials
Gandharvas, *Vidyadharas*, *Kinnaras*, and *Apsaras*,
The Masters of the Arts.

Unbearable was the form of Ahi,
Horror manifest.
Those sensitive ones, immersed in *Rasa*

In dread forgot their callings
Music, stories, love, and dance;
The world of Vritra had no place for the exquisite.

Vritra smashed the shades and the grottos,
He shattered the platforms and the halls,
He scarred the peaks with his talons;
The flaming cincture created by the Serpent's path
Turned the golden hue of Mount Meru
Black with the charred remains of Artists.

Still Vritra rose higher.

Finally piercing through the thick clouds
He went beyond the sky of the living
Spiralling about the pure diamond peak of Meru
Stretching towards an infinity
Unseen by any mortal eye but his.

Untiring,
He rose and rose,
Until he arrived at the eternal gardens –
The verdant *Nandana*,
Idyll of the *Devatas*.

In that place of everlasting spring
The Great Serpent burnt down *Kalpataru*,

The wish-granting tree,
Unleashing the taint of nightmares
On the dreams of all mortals.

Airavata, the great white elephant
Many headed mount of Indra,
Charged at Vritra, shuddering in rage;
Yet with one swipe of his tail
The Great Serpent cast him down into the ocean.

Nandana, engulfed in flames, resembled an inferno.
Forty-eight thousand *Brahmarshis* left that abode
Along with the countless *Siddhas* who inhabited *Svarga*;
Some sought refuge in the stars
Others in distant forests and devout wombs.

Drained of the austerities of those who knew *Brahman*,
Svarga resembled the altar of a failed *Yajna*;
The *Parijaat* flowers lost their fragrance
The *Kaamdhenu* lost her peace
A damp winter engulfed the heavens.

Finally, Vritra appeared at the gates of Amaravati,
The city of the Immortals,
The home of the Devatas;
No foe had ever breached its walls
No shadow had ever darkened its glades.

Yet black darkness did Vritra unleash
As he towered above the thousand-pillared hall;
He smashed the ground again and again,
Each shockwave a challenge to the murderer of
  Trishira –
It was time for the reckoning.

In grim silence,
The *Devatas* and the *Maruts* streamed out;
The Great Serpent, that wrath of vengeance,
Flew up, encircling the devastated *Svarga*,
And rained down fire and poison on the immortals.

Stern were their faces as they hurled their weapons,
Only to watch them bounce off, harmless,
Their immortal strength failing against Ahi's
  adamantine skin;
Yet ever stronger did Vritra grow
As he absorbed the power of the *Devata's* attacks.

With an angry roar Indra attacked his foe,
But the Great Serpent scarcely flinched;
Hapless against that unfathomable calamity
The immortals were but lifeless props
In the stage play of their own doom.

Howling with rage,
Ahi rampaged across *Svarga*

His hatred crashing against everything the *Devatas*
had built.
Stone by stone and brick by brick,
He shattered Amaravati into pitiful rubble.

Then finally, the rampant Ahi grabbed Indra,
Picking him up like a child's doll.
Unflinching in hatred,
The terrifying one severed his senses
And reduced Indra to mere Purandara.

When he lost his eyes,
Purandara was cut off from the light of *Ushas*.
When he lost his ears,
Purandara was cut off from the chants of *Rishis*.
When he lost his nose,
Purandara was cut off from the smell of rain.
When he lost his tongue,
Purandara was cut off from the taste of *Soma*.
When he lost his skin,
Purandara was cut off from the fields left fallow.

In that helpless state,
Purandara had no thought but self-preservation
No understanding but pain
No awareness but ego
And no emotion but fear;
The once King of the *Devatas* had been reduced

To the barest sliver of life
To have ever existed in the three worlds.

For a moment it seemed
As if the Great Serpent would swallow him whole,
But then Ahi yawned,
Disinterested all of a sudden;
With a final glance, filled with disgust
He threw away the writhing remains of Purandara.

His vengeance complete,
Vritra roared again and again;
Halfway around the world
Tvashta and Virochana heard his joy
And once more began to weep for Vishvarupa.

On seeing their King thus defeated
The *Devatas* and the *Maruts* retreated in terror;
The Great Serpent curled his body around *Svarga*
And exerting immense pressure,
Crushed the diamond peak of Meru
Into a supernova of glittering jewels.

Across the earth,
Mortals shuddered
At the sight of flaming meteors,
Beyond count,
Howling down a broken sky

Piercing the dark clouds with rainbow scars,
Crashing upon the lower slopes of Meru.

Those shards of burning diamonds
Shattered upon impact,
Covering the sky with sharp splinters
As if a volley of arrows had been fired
From the most expensive quiver ever.

Then came the earthquakes and the landslides.
The ground heaved and groaned
Boulders ground against each other in the frenzied mud
Toppling upon themselves to form a grotesque barrier
Blocking the path of the rivers which gushed into the plains.

Then, like a spectre from the darkest nightmare
The immense form of Vritra
Emerged from the swirling gloom,
Slowly slithering down the mountain.

On that shattered Meru
Vritra finally decided to rest;
Slowly he coiled his massive form
Amidst the debris of his destruction.

When he looked down
Surveying the desolation he had wrought

His smile was gentle,
And his eyes peaceful.

The waters of the world weakened to a drip,
And then ceased to flow.

Svarga had fallen.
The *Devatas* had lost.
A crack appeared across the old order.

The world became a different place.

The *Kaleyas* cheered in delight.
The mortals shuddered in terror.

A whisper was then heard by all who breathed.

My Song of Freedom (*Vritra*)

Once there was an unwanted baby
Abandoned by her whore mother
Unknown to her lecher father,
She cried and cried until she couldn't anymore;
When she died of hunger
Stray dogs ate her flesh
Whilst you, my beloved subjects,
Held your crinkled nose to block out the stench.

You quickened your pace,
You gulped down your bitter bile,
Swiftly averting your disgusted gaze
You walked away, planning your lunch.

Be proud, you did well.

Will you believe in the sadistic *Law of Karma*
Which says that the baby deserved her fate?

Do not be scared to admit
What you already know to be true in your heart-
There is no good.
There is no bad.
Nothing is sacred in this random world.

Things happen.
Nothing matters.
Nobody cares.
Everything is meaningless.
You are on your own.
Dharma is a lie.

The *Devatas* too won't matter–
Not now,
And not ever in the future;
I have vanquished them all.

Yes indeed, I have destroyed Indra,
His gibbous greed shall wax no more.

Forget that they ever existed.

Deny them your worship and faith,
Until they forever leave your minds
Their one last hope of refuge;
Let the *Devatas* flee with their baggage –
Self-indulgent rituals,
Oppressive expectations,
Arbitrary rules,
Stifling duty.
Let their total defeat unshackle you
From the chains of turgid morality
And the suffocating reek of hypocrisy.

I am the Lord of Meaninglessness,
I free you all from the tyranny of Order.

Welcome to my world;
No boundaries shall hold you back here
No horizon will be too far
No heaven out of your reach –
Now you are free
Now you are you,
Only you,
And nothing else but you.

The Sutradhar Speaks

Time passed, like it always does.

When the *Devatas* were lost and powerless
When humanity became ashamed of their *Dharma*,
Their sacred bond was shattered;
The path to Meru lay forgotten,
And no human dared to embrace the *Way of the Aarya*.

The form of Vritra slowly became imperceptible;
The *Kaleyas* dispersed,
Finding dark hiding places
In the deepest recesses of human instinct.

As that day of terror slowly faded from our memory,
Yet life, as it always does,
Against all odds,
Found a way to thrive.

This was the triumph of Vritra;
A world living under his shadow –
Seduced by his thoughts
Corrupted by his minions
Yet blissfully unaware of his existence.

4| DOOMSCROLLING A FORSAKEN TIMELINE

One (*Voices Unseen*)

The engines of industry
Belched rancid black smoke.

Far from the city lights
By the shores of a dead river,
Tiptoeing on crumbling leaves,
The last *Bharatnatyam* dancer
Put on a tattered gas mask
For her final dance.

She died amidst the barren tree trunks,
Taking *Bharatnatyam* with her.

A single teardrop
Penetrated her leaky, useless facade,
To hopelessly fall on the parched ground
And disappear.

Two (*The Sutradhar*)

There used to be an ordinary village
With a hundred houses
Dotted around a beautiful lake.

When Vritra blocked the mountain waters
The land was ravaged by drought,

But the villagers refused to share their water;
The harder the times became,
The more the village prospered.

Years passed by.
The lake finally began to dry out.

Ties of blood and years of friendship
Were forgotten in days;
Snarling and scheming,
Each villager hoarded all they could
For themselves, and themselves alone.

Once the lake became empty.
When all the food ran out,
They began to eat each other.

Then one night the raiders came.

The villagers hid in their homes
Cowering in fear as the walls closed in.
One by one,
The raiders butchered them all,
And left.

<u>Three (*Voices Unseen*)</u>

A whispering ghost lived on a tree;

It murmured powerful nonsense
To seduce folks who rested in the shade.

Hypnotized by his innuendo
Those travellers became his slaves
Repeating those very same words
To enslave their own.

The ghost divided his slaves into armies,
And made them fight each other.

Roaming the battlefields at night,
The whispering ghost feasted.

Four (*The Sutradhar*)

On a vast frozen plain,
A hungry hunter caught three birds
Too weak to fly away.
Under the stars, he made a fire
But when the time came,
Pity overcame his famished heart.

He freed the birds.

The four of them hunched around that tiny fire
Scarce respite from the dark, bitter cold;

Before the hunter passed,
He whispered –
"Eat me, O birds, and live."
The birds snuggled up instead
To his still-warm corpse.

In the morning chill,
The fire died
And the birds waited.

Five (*Voices Unseen*)

Clutching the *murti* served by his ancestors
The frail old priest fled.

Demonic laughter filled the air,
The filthy sound of a cancerous orgy
Celebrating rape and rapine;
Frenzied idol breakers,
Barely human,
Senseless with zeal,
Chanting the name of their god,
Chased the priest
To the banks of river Tungabhadra.

With nowhere left to run
The priest, defiant till the end,
Jumped into the deep,
Cradling his beloved God.

The waters received him,
Just like a mother protects her son,
And then flowed on, unbothered,
Confounding the maniacs.

Six (*The Sutradhar*)

A mad king once said,
"The world is upside down."

His ministers danced around their insane master.

Yes, your majesty!
Indeed, nothing is as it seems!
Right is wrong!
Rules are oppression!
Strength is weakness!
Men are women!
Enemies are friends!
Honour is toxic!
Oh, what a misunderstood world we live in!

So, the mad king made a rule
That there were to be no rules
And anyone against that rule
Was a rule breaker,
To be condemned to death.

Anarchy descended –
Words lost their meaning,
Actions had no consequences,
There remained nothing to hold on to;
So, they all fought among themselves,
Until the country was no more.

Who knows what happened to the mad king;
Everyone else was either dead or a slave.

Seven (*Voices Unseen*)

A mother wandered into a place of slaughter
Searching for her dead kids
Who fought against each other
Until bitter death.

She was shunned by all.
Branding her a traitor,
Each side blamed her for failing her children;
They called her a bad mother.

Then, outside one nameless camp,
Someone killed her,
Driven by furious disgust,
Then left the body in the no man's land.

Time went by.
The warring armies made peace.

Sunlight bleached the mother's bones
Just like those of her unclaimed kids.

Eight (*The Sutradhar*)

On the first morning
After the last day of work,
The jobless employee woke up
In a stranger's home,
And knew not what to do.

Walking out of the door was familiar.
The streets too, were familiar.
He went to a familiar market,
Walked by the racks filled with *Wonderful*,
But knew not what to buy.

As he stood by the road,
No longer a part of the endless traffic
He counted a thousand unknown alleys
Just beside the one which took him home,
And he knew not where to go.

He stayed where he was
Overwhelmed and undecided;
A t-shirt walked by,
Who am I?
He knew not what to say.

Nine (*The Sutradhar and the Voices Unseen*)

A little girl chanced upon an abandoned temple.

She saw beautiful sculptures
Of dancing maidens adorning the walls;
When she studied their poses
The stones became her teachers,
Whispering in her ears the mysteries of *Karanas*.

People laughed,
And people mocked,
And people screamed in her face,
Enraged at her love for that secret, forgotten world.

Ignoring their jealous pettiness
She threw away all her chains –
The visible ones,
Along with the ones unseen,
To just keep dancing and dancing,
In that lonely abandoned temple
Under the stony eyes of her ancient tutors,
All by herself,
To a rhythm that only she could hear
For an audience that even she could not see
Until one glorious day,
Just for her,
Bharatnatyam came alive once again.

5| ZERO

Purandara Speaks

I was alone,
Surrounded by absolute darkness.

No.

To be very honest,
I didn't even know that it was dark
For I had not yet seen what light looked like
Nor did I understand the meaning of loneliness;
The truth is, I hardly knew who or what *'I'* was.

At first, there was only stillness.

Inert and ignorant,
Little did I realize
That I was standing on the edge of a precipice.

When movement came,
My first faltering step
(Or did I feel a push?)
Threw me down
Into the bottomless abyss.

I fell, and fell, and fell.

I kept falling,
Until, in my cocoon of black nothingness

I lost all acuity –
Motion and stillness melded into one.

Then a tiny speck of light
Shyly appeared
Just out of reach.
I named it Dhruva,
The Star of the North.

Pulled by cold starlight
I flew towards Dhruva,
Brighter and brighter it grew
Until I could not look anymore.
Our collision shattered that star
Into countless tiny suns
Each more luminous than its brother,
Overwhelming my senses
With a cacophony of light.

As I hurtled past churning nebulae
Becoming ever more lost
In the dazzling maze of feeble starspawn
And the cul-de-sac of extravagant galaxies
I realized that I was not who I previously was –
Not anymore.

Time, energy, and matter were now intruders
To what was once my own personal universe.

Confronted with wonder beyond understanding
My mind began to construct its own pattern of reality
Bracing my sanity to the empyrean milestones
Which punctuated the barely perceptible,
Yet endless emptiness just beyond my vision.

It was good while it lasted.

Then the spectacle was spent;
The lights went out.

Once more I was floating in the dark
Utterly powerless and inert,
Tethered to an invisible puppeteer.
Yet somehow, the faintest flicker of yearning
Made me cling to the memory of that cosmic dance
Which burnt so brightly in my consciousness;
I welcomed the pain,
Desperate not to lose myself once again
To the stifling stillness of the past.

I wanted to see the light again.

This was… desire
Precious,
Fiery,
Living.

I had to see the light again.

Like an ache in the chest
Like unwept tears
Like a titan in a net
Like a love not to be
My desire grew and grew
Compounded by time
Until it broke through the dam of my impotence
Shattering the constraints of my feeble shell
Banishing forever the primordial stillness.

I was not powerless anymore.

From Darkness to the Light, I will go.
The light was the truth,
All else was false.

Pain.
Joy.
Freedom.
I took a deep breath,
Finally whole again.

I had found myself.

From Untruth to the Supreme Truth I will go.

I opened my eyes
On the fragrant shore of the ocean of bliss
And threw myself at the lotus feet of MahaVishnu.

From Decay to Eternal Life, I will go.

PART FIVE

AMRITA

The Sutradhar wears the mask of
sunlight through rain clouds.

1| THE OUTSTRETCHED HAND OF MERCY

The Sutradhar Speaks

It was not a world for the weak.

Under the rainless skies,
The world suffered.

Fuelled by Vritra's fierce gaze
The merciless drought raged across the world;
It sapped all strength,
It sucked all will,
It drained everything,
Leaving behind just a parched husk,
So that breathing itself felt like a tax.

Slowly, meaning seeped out from the wounds of the world.

Now a cadaver drained of blood
The shock of reality made humanity twitch
Uncontrolled, erratic, random –
And people thought that itself was the truth of existence,
That reality was, in fact, meaningless.

Oh, how the world suffered!

When meaning was lost,
When the *Way of the Aarya* was extinct,

Conflict raged everywhere;
In the minds of men and women,
On the streets and the ghettos,
In gilded chambers with high tables,
Within humble kitchens and dark bedrooms.

Men turned against Life,
Religions rose against *Dharma*
Rulers plotted against their own people
The people whispered against their neighbours,
The neighbours betrayed their own blood,
Until they all convinced themselves
That their warped vision was timeless wisdom.

It was always thus.
Our history is conflict.
Our nature is conflict.
Being alive itself is conflict.

It was always thus,
We cannot imagine any other way,
We cannot imagine a better world,
So, it was always thus.

Decorated with honeyed words,
Selfishness was exalted to a virtue,
And with its practice,
Came the gift of loneliness.

The words of Vritra rang true –
Everyone was alone,
Everyone had to fend for themselves.

Sounds familiar?
Never mind.

Oh, it was not a world for the weak!

In *Vaikuntha*,
Vishnu's realm of infinite joy
Purandara woke up;
That fallen Indra
With folded hands
Begged for assistance
From the almighty Narayana.

Purandara Speaks

In utter shame, I stand before you.

Drunk with arrogance
I insulted our teacher;
The wise Brihaspati left Amaravati,
Predicting our fall.

Then Tvashta's ascetic son
Fell prey to my anger;

When I decapitated that three-headed one
The sin of *Brahmahatya* took away my strength.

Defeated by the mighty Vritra,
The *Devatas* were driven away from *Svarga;*
Lost in the wilderness beyond man's thoughts,
They shiver, pitiful, and powerless.

The *Kaleyas* control this broken world
Where Vritra's aura distorts reality,
Shunning their duties as oppression
People take their rights for granted.

Listen to the triumphant laughter of Ahi's minions,
Seeding corruption across the worlds;
Vritra has held back the waters,
There is no more rain.

In the absence of nature's bounty
A great darkness consumes mankind,
The way of Dharma is forgotten;
Like cannibals, nations devour each other.

Fear controls the hearts of the living;
The rabid mob has become the law,
Wisdom is now a crime
Logic and respect, taboo.

When their lives get divorced from nature
The mortals lose sight of *Rta*.
Inevitably, the *Law of the Fish*
Holds sway over civilization.

Help us, O Jagannatha!
Let me redeem myself!
Lend your strength to my arms
So that I may confront the monstrous Ahi
To free the waters of the world.

If that is not your wish, O Protector,
Take birth yourself!
Bring back meaning to the world
Smite this *Asura* with your own hands,
Establish another golden age.

Vishnu Speaks

What you speak is truth,
But only a half-truth.

The path to redemption is difficult, Purandara.

Mired in *Adharma* your actions have been.
Reduced to a bundle of the same human failings
Whose prayers you enjoyed so very much –
Selfish and self-important you became,

Losing control of your senses,
A slave to your basest self
Unworthy of your throne.

Neither awareness nor guilt
Gives relief from the burden of *Karma*;
The fruits of your deeds
Will land on your head
Uncompromising,
No matter who you are
No matter how you feel.

Indeed, by what right do you claim redemption?

How can you think of defeating Vritra
When you have not defeated
Your own pride,
Your own entitlement?

Who are the *Kaleyas*
If not the stark reflection
Of your own excesses
Indulged with brazen impunity?

How else was Vritra born
If not from the coupling of fear and power,
The twin fig leaves of *Adharma*
Each sustaining the other?

Is not the awful form of Ahi,
The collapsed ruin
Of a sick Svarga
Burdened by your schemes and deceit?

Purandara Speaks

All that you speak is true;

Yes, I am worthy of punishment!
Yes, the *Devatas* failed!

But does your heart not weep
To see the misery of the people
Under the rule of Vritra?

Vishnu Speaks

Do not be worried about the world of men;
They will survive without you,
They will prosper without you,
And they may even rediscover
That which they call *Dharma*,
Without your assistance.

When the *Devatas* were too frail
To answer the piteous cries
Of those toiling millions

Scratching the parched earth,
Of those hungry ones
Who create life to feed life –
Humanity did not roll over and die.

A few gave up,
Disheartened;
But others drew upon their *Purushartha*,
With their intelligence and industry
They worked hard and built their engines
Failing and trying again and again,
Until they thought they had tamed nature
By their own strength,
In their own, unique way.

Look at the grand civilization they have built,
Marvel at its wonders!

Channelling the power of the *Devatas* themselves
They have flown across the skies,
They have broken the atom;
Curing the incurable
They have stepped on the moon,
And shrunk the entire world
To fit into their palms!

Without even knowing Vritra,
They have survived him so far.

Tell me, Purandara,
Is it not better to let them be?

Purandara Speaks

But are they happy, my Lord?

Vishnu Speaks

You are asking the wrong question.

It is the nature of man to challenge the gods;
The will to defy is what makes one human.
Yet, the price of happiness for humanity
Cannot be the death of everyone else.

O Purandara! Understand this,
Humanity has never lacked power
But only the wisdom to wield it.

This was the task you failed,
The very purpose of the *Way of the Aarya* –
To ensure the safety of the whole natural order,
So that all life flourishes
So that every being is in harmony
So that none is exploited
So that the powerless does not fall prey to greed
So that humanity becomes the guardian of *Rta*
And not the master of the world.

Now, in the age of the Great Serpent,
Humanity,
Drunk with its own prosperity,
Has turned its back to the Way of the Aarya;
Willingly seduced by the illusion of freedom
Offered by the many voices of the *Kaleyas*,
It has rejected the bounds of *Purushartha*
Which had once led them to greatness
But now felt like an obsolete barrier,
A meaningless check against their unbridled ambitions.

Thus, having lost sight
Of their own purpose and meaning
Today humans think of others as lesser beings,
To be exploited, enslaved or monetized
Or to be put in a golden cage,
To be showered with pity
Or suffocated by cloying concern
But never to be ceded any real agency,
Never to be given any real respect.

Acolytes of the Serpent,
Decadent hoarders emulating their master,
Coil around their vast riches
Never enough,
Never satisfied,
Slowly sucking the world dry
Poisoning the air, the earth, and the sea
In their relentless war against nature.

Their brainwashed minions
Seething with cynicism,
Perpetually malcontent,
Invert all that is real,
Seeking pleasure in imagined victimhood;
Unable to tell right from wrong
The foolish ones with the shrillest screams
Drown out common sense with gibberish
To infect humanity
With bitter divisions and absurd laws.

If I were to take birth
Perhaps it would not be for the deliverance
Of humans and their corrupt civilization,
But as an instrument of *Karma,*
To protect and preserve nature
To restore the cosmic order
And bring humanity to justice
For their transgressions
Against the tapestry of life.

The world is not a garden,
Humanity is not a gardener;
No, this universe is a forest of life
Each of us precious and unique
Each of us a part of the whole
None a lord over another
All of them, a part of each other.

Yet, much that is good endures in the world of men;
Embedded in their deep subconscious
Instincts from their *Aarya* past lie in wait
Breaking free gloriously time after time –
Often unbidden
Often by the call of circumstance
Often through the practice of hallowed tradition,
Often by walking forgotten paths in truest ignorance.

The compassionate ones
The seekers of science
The keepers of knowledge
The ones who feed others
The friends in the final journey
And countless such great souls;
For their sake, I will show mercy for now
And give humans one final chance.

So, I shall whisper in your ears
The key to the riddle of Vritra,
In the hope that your final battle
Changes the fortune of the mortal world.

Go, and give humanity purpose, Purandara!
Reforge the sacred bond between *Devatas* and humans
Remind the world once again
The virtues and delights
Of the *Way of the Aarya*.

Infuse each of their lives with meaning again,
Reveal to them once more the wonder of this universe
Show them the tapestry of interconnected life,
And remind them of their gifts and responsibilities.

Bring all things living
Back under the sweet shade of *Dharma*.

Let humanity become *Aarya* once again.

2| IN THE LABYRINTH

The Sutradhar Speaks

Head bowed,
His entire being burning with remorse
Purandara knelt before
Yet another sage he had murdered.

Gentle was the breeze at the hermitage of Dadhichi;
Untouched by Vritra's drought,
It was a realm of unfailing light
In a world full of sorrow and decay.

The energy of the meditating *Rishi*
Incinerated all delusions;
Purandara finally understood
What being weak meant.

His throat was parched
His eyes watered
His ears buzzed
His hands, clasped in prayer, trembled.

Thus, in great torment he wept
Alone and pathetic,
In front of a gigantic *Asvattha* tree,
And thus, he was found
By Suvarchas the virtuous.

That kind-hearted lady,
Wife of the radiant Dadhichi
That ancient sage who knew the secrets
The one who remembered the *Devatas* and Vritra,
Could not recognize Purandara,
Reduced to that pitiful state.

Suvarchas Speaks

Who are you child?
Why do you weep?
What causes you distress?
How can we help you?

Come, let me wipe your tears;
Rest a little.
Eat these fresh fruits from the forest.
Drink this nectar-like water from the stream.
Once you gain control of your senses
The *Rishi* will speak to you.

Purandara Speaks

Alas, Mother!
Know me to be the guilty one
Who once robbed you of your light,
Know me to be the shameless one,
Who is again the harbinger of sorrow,

Know me to be the selfish one
Maddened in pursuit of violence and power;
Know me to be the wretched Purandara,
Once Indra,
Now a humble beggar
Seeking your husband's charity.

Suvarchas Speaks

O Purandara! O Indra!
My son!
Why are you in this miserable state?
Why do you speak in this cryptic manner?
Why do you call yourself guilty?

The Sutradhar Speaks

Unable to answer,
Or to meet the gaze of Suvarchas
Purandara stared at the ground,
Powerless,
Incapable of uttering a single word.

When the shadows lengthened,
Sage Dadhichi came out of his thoughts;
Witnessing the tableau in front of him,
His eyes twinkled
For that descendant of Bhrigu
Already knew what Purandara was seeking.

Rishi Dadhichi Speaks

Let the past remain in the past,
Let us not cause unnecessary worry
To my innocent wife.
O Purandara, tell me,
Why have you visited my humble abode?

Purandara Speaks

I come bearing the message of MahaVishnu,
The protector of the worlds.
When I sought his help
To defeat the terrifying Vritra
And end his age of torment,
He sent me to you.

"Go to the illustrious Rishi Dadhichi
Beg for his forgiveness
And seek refuge in his compassion;
He will understand what is to be done."

Yet when I arrived,
My guilt,
For the enormity of my crime against you
Sealed my lips;
There can be no redemption for me.

Let me depart in peace.

Rishi Dadhichi Speaks

Wait!
You don't get to escape your Karma so easily;
How can one who was once Indra
Give such sorry excuses
To avoid doing what must be done?

How can one
With such weak will
Serve the purpose of MahaVishnu
And shoulder the burden
To re-establish *Dharma* on earth?

Purandara Speaks

So, will you forgive me then?

Rishi Dadhichi Speaks

It is easy to seek forgiveness from me;
Go, seek forgiveness from those
Who you looked down upon
Thinking they were beneath your station.

Go, seek out the Ashvin Twins,
The one who is white and the one who is tawny –
Go find those horse-headed celestials,
The *Nasatyas*,

The supreme friends of the mortals,
The patrons of medicine and safe returns.

Cast out by you long ago
Those two remained unharmed
When Vritra had attacked *Swarga*,
Even now they roam unseen,
A sanctuary to the suffering
Always healing, always helping
Always resisting the poison of the *Kaleyas*.

Find them!
Seek strength from their knowledge
Which you had once so violently opposed,
So that you may become worthy again
Of becoming an instrument of *Dharma*!

Purandara Speaks

And doing this will help me defeat Vritra?

Rishi Dadhichi Speaks

I know the Will of MahaVishnu;
I know how you can defeat the Great Serpent
And pull back the curtain of darkness
Which has descended upon this earth.

But what are you now,
But a fallow field, Purandara?

Weak in body and spirit,
My words will pass through your mind
Like water poured on a sieve.

You must grow strong.

Forged anew in body and spirit,
By the unrelenting fires of *tapas*
You will have to rise above your *indriya*
And once more take an oath
To fulfil your responsibilities,
And repay your debts-
To the eternal *Brahman*,
To the knowledge of the *Rishis*,
To the virtuous *Ancestors*
To the civilization of *Dharma*
To the order of *Nature*.

Thus, you shall become a true Indra again,
Just as it had once happened before,
When the mysteries of the universe
Were first revealed to the human gaze.

O Purandara! Let this be your path!
Complete your penance,
Return to me once this task is done;
Only then shall you receive
The power to destroy Ahi.

3| A DROP OF HONEY IN MY PALMS

The Sutradhar Speaks

All things are impermanent.
All lives will decay
All kingdoms will crumble
All palaces will turn to dust,
All pride will reduce to ashes;
Time will devour all,
Nothing will remain
Nothing will endure
Except the shining, shimmering *Aatman*,
Merging into the infinite, boundless *Brahman*.

Indra once ruled the clouds
He called down the rains
Smote his foes with lighting;
Shattering the cities of his enemies
He roamed proudly,
Drunk with *Soma*,
Resplendent in the company of his fierce *Maruts* –
But then he fell.

Losing everything,
He became *Purandara*.

Purandara Speaks

Brought down by my arrogance,
Cast out from my home,

Abandoned by my peers
Vilified by my followers,
I have lost everything,
I have let everyone down;
What am I but a disappointment?

The Ballad of a Powerless God (*Voices Unseen and Purandara*)

I found a little girl
Defiled, devoured, and ravaged
Dying by the side of a nameless road;
I sat weeping beside him.

Not once did she call out for help
To either man or God.
In the Age of Vritra,
Even little girls know that prayers are futile.

Without opening her eyes
She died
And the powerless Purandara wept...
Powerlessly.

What is the cure of my helpless rage?
Where is hope in this wretched world?
How do I soothe their endless pain?
Oh, what a curse my weakness is,
What a curse weakness is!

Rummage through your empty chest,
Take stock of the treasures lost
Let your fingers feel the worn contours
Of a long discarded basic truth –
Only when you are left with nothing,
Will you be free of your fears.

You must walk the Path of Penitence.

The Sutradhar Speaks

Purandara became a seeker.

Like a dying tree thirsts for water,
Purandara now sought mercy
From those he had once disdained
When wielding supreme power.

In the fields and the mountains
By the sands of the seas
Under the blazing sun of the desert
Amidst the monsoons torrents
Among the heaving, crushing crowds
Inhabiting the dusty streets of *Bharata*,
He wandered,
A mystic,
Searching for the horse-headed twins,
Clinging on to the words of Dadhichi.

No, he did not find them.
Instead, he met the people.

For the very first time,
He spoke to us as an equal;
Away from the fire of the sacrifices
Away from the chants of the *Vedas*
Away from the music of the celebrations
Away from the surrender devotion
Away from the tears of prayer
Away from even the comfort of recognition.

When we spoke,
He came to know us,
Like he had never known us before –
Back when he was up in the skies
To bless us with rains,
Or invited to the *Yajna*
To grant us success.

The more he knew us,
The more Purandara felt one with us;
The more he felt one with us
The more he forgot himself,
Until he even forgot what he was searching for.

The years passed;
Purandara roamed the world,

Meeting every one of us.

Of course, I met him too.
Just like you did.
Yes, you.
Don't you remember?

He was an earthworm
When you tilled the land;
And he granted you Wisdom.
Don't you remember his words?

To all things the Earth is Honey,
All things are Honey to the Earth;
The radiant, eternal being in Earth,
And the radiant, eternal being
Present in this body as Matter,
Are both Honey.

That being is Aatman.
That being is Amrita.
That being is Brahman.
That being is All.

He was a fish
When you were a fisherman;
And he granted you Wisdom.
Don't you remember his words?

To all things the Water is Honey,
All things are Honey to the Water;
The radiant, eternal being in Water,
And the radiant, eternal being
Present in this body as Seed,
Are both Honey.

That being is Aatman.
That being is Amrita.
That being is Brahman.
That being is All.

He was firewood
When you were a priest;
And he granted you Wisdom.
Don't you remember his words?

To all things the Fire is Honey,
All things are Honey to the Fire;
The radiant, eternal being in Fire,
And the radiant, eternal being
Present in this body as Speech,
Are both Honey.

That being is Aatman.
That being is Amrita.
That being is Brahman.
That being is All.

He was an eagle
When you were a hunter;
And he granted you Wisdom.
Don't you remember his words?

To all things the Air is Honey,
All things are Honey to the Air;
The radiant, eternal being in Air,
And the radiant, eternal being
Present in this body as Life,
Are both Honey.

That being is Aatman.
That being is Amrita.
That being is Brahman.
That being is All.

He was a firefly
When you were blind;
And he granted you Wisdom.
Don't you remember his words?

To all things the Sun is Honey,
All things are Honey to the Sun;
The radiant, eternal being in Sun,
And the radiant, eternal being
Present in this body as Vision,
Are both Honey.

That being is Aatman.
That being is Amrita.
That being is Brahman.
That being is All.

He was a star
When you were lost;
And he granted you Wisdom.
Don't you remember his words?

To all things the Directions are Honey,
All things are Honey to the Directions;
The radiant, eternal being in the Directions,
And the radiant, eternal being
Present in this body as Hearing,
Are both Honey.

That being is Aatman.
That being is Amrita.
That being is Brahman.
That being is All.

He was your loneliness
When you found yourself alone;
And he granted you Wisdom.
Don't you remember his words?

To all things the Moon is Honey,
All things are Honey to the Moon;

The radiant, eternal being in the Moon,
And the radiant, eternal being
Present in this body as the Mind,
Are both Honey.

That being is Aatman.
That being is Amrita.
That being is Brahman.
That being is All.

He was your bloodlust
When you were a warrior;
And he granted you Wisdom.
Don't you remember his words?

To all things the Lightning is Honey,
All things are Honey to the Lightning;
The radiant, eternal being in the Lightning,
And the radiant, eternal being
Present in this body as Energy,
Are both Honey.

That being is Aatman.
That being is Amrita.
That being is Brahman.
That being is All.

He was your mother tongue
When you found your speech;

And he granted you Wisdom.
Don't you remember his words?

To all things the Thunder is Honey,
All things are Honey to the Thunder;
The radiant, eternal being in the Thunder,
And the radiant, eternal being
Present in this body as Sound,
Are both Honey.

That being is Aatman.
That being is Amrita.
That being is Brahman.
That being is All.

He was infinity
When you first defied gravity;
And he granted you Wisdom.
Don't you remember his words?

To all things the Sky is Honey,
All things are Honey to the Sky;
The radiant, eternal being in the Sky,
And the radiant, eternal being
Present in this body as the Heart,
Are both Honey.

That being is Aatman.
That being is Amrita.

That being is Brahman.
That being is All.

He was patience
When you were ready to give up;
And he granted you Wisdom.
Don't you remember his words?

To all things Dharma is Honey,
All things are Honey to Dharma;
The radiant, eternal being in Dharma,
And the radiant, eternal being
Present in this body as the Righteous Conduct,
Are both Honey.

That being is Aatman.
That being is Amrita.
That being is Brahman.
That being is All.

He was your hand
When you lit your first pyre;
And he granted you Wisdom.
Don't you remember his words?

To all things Truth is Honey,
All things are Honey to Truth;
The radiant, eternal being in Truth,
And the radiant, eternal being

Present in this body as Truth,
Are both Honey.

That being is Aatman.
That being is Amrita.
That being is Brahman.
That being is All.

He was your child
When you first saw their smile;
And he granted you Wisdom.
Don't you remember his words?

To all things Humanity is Honey,
All things are Honey to Humanity;
The radiant, eternal being in Humanity,
And the radiant, eternal being
Present in this body as Humanity,
Are both Honey.

That being is Aatman.
That being is Amrita.
That being is Brahman.
That being is All.

He is the final voice
You will hear just before you die;
And he will grant you Wisdom.
Don't you remember his words?

To all things Aatman is Honey,
All things are Honey to Aatman;
The radiant, eternal being in Aatman,
And the radiant, eternal being
Present in this body as Aatman,
Are both Honey.

That being is Aatman.
That being is Amrita.
That being is Brahman.
That being is All.

Let us forgive Purandara,
The one who has revealed to us
This Wisdom which is honey,
This Wisdom which breaks all shackles,
This Wisdom which leads to *Moksha*.

Everlasting,
All encompassing,
The Aatman rules all,
The Aatman is the king of everything;
All beings
All Devatas
All worlds
All lives
Every single thing
Is established in the Aatman,
Timeless,

Eternal,
Brahman.

Voices Unseen

Let Purandara confess to the world.
Let Purandara state his goals.
Let Purandara seek forgiveness.
Let Purandara find forgiveness.

Let him find peace.
Let him find peace.
Let him find peace.

My Shame (*Purandara*)

Dadhichi *Atharvan* knew *The Secret of Honey*;
Some say I revealed it to him,
Some say the *Grandfather* did.
Fearful of the power that knowledge could grant,
I warned the Sage to not divulge this secret
With the threat of decapitation.

The Ashvins,
Shunned and reviled by me
Were especially forbidden
To pursue this knowledge;
Yet they went to Dadhichi

And begged him,
For the sake of the living world,
To accept them as his students.

Those wondrous physicians
Cut off Dadhichi's head,
Replacing it with that of a horse;
Then that horse headed being,
Asvashira,
Taught the Ashvins *The Secret of Honey*.

Shuddering with rage,
I arrived at the hermitage;
I swung my blade
To cut off the head of *Asvashira*,
Whereupon the Ashvin twins
Quickly reattaching his original head
Brought Dadhichi back to life.

Thus did knowledge escape my jealous prison of threats.

I am Vritra.
I blocked knowledge
Just like Vritra has blocked the waters.
I cast out the Ashvins
Just like Vritra cast me out.
Tell me, am I not Ahi?

I have no right to absolution.
I will walk the endless Path of Penitence.

The Sutradhar Speaks

Rise up from the depths, O King!

Remember *The Secret of Honey.*
Remember who you are.
By your own grace,
Through your own remembrance,
Go beyond forgiveness,
Go beyond redemption,
Embrace the *Yoga* of duty,
Become Indra again.

Plant your feet on this ground which is real
Fill your lungs with this air which is real
Recall yourself, and roar once more!
Let the world know that *Adharma* is real!
Let the world know that *Dharma* too, is real!
Vanquish Vritra,
Free the world of the Serpent's drought,
Rise with the *Aaryas* once more.

Rise!
Rise!
Rise!

Voices Unseen

Let his deeds free Purandara from the Path of Penitence.

May he find peace.

The Promise (*Purandara*)

My deeds will free me from the Path of Penitence.

I will not seek forgiveness.
Duty will be my *Karma*.

Powerless though I am
I shall be at your side,
And by the side of every mortal
Human, animal, plant, bird, fish and everyone else.

Through your struggles I will struggle,
Through your suffering I will suffer,
And when you close your eyes,
You will find my shoulders a place of rest.

For as long as it takes, I will be there by your side.

Naked, stripped of all my pretensions
I will look into my own eyes
Reflected in yours;

In embracing you,
I will embrace myself –
Fully aware,
Without any regrets,
Finally at peace with my essential nature.

When all my debts are paid, I will be reborn.

Then we shall defeat Vritra.
Then we shall proclaim *Dharma*.
Then we shall know peace.

4| SOMETHING GREATER THAN ME

The Storm King (*Voices Unseen*)

I am a stranger with a stranger's face
I have no country, I have no place
Without a history, without any roots
I have no culture, I have no grace.

The quicksand pulls me ever down
The more I struggle, the more I drown
Garbage stains my mind and dreams
All alone, I struggle to breathe.

In such times he used to come
Drunk and ruddy his glowing form
Untamed and pure as the monsoon rain
Dragging me towards the start again.

Uprooting trees and flooding earth
Unreasonable his red-eyed wrath
With thunder did he settle the score
With violence did he clean the slate.

Yet clear was his laughter heard
When lightning flashed above the earth
Oh, where did our Storm King go?
Where did our Storm King go?

Why was that fire quenched
Why did the storm get tamed

Why did his fury calm
Why did he understand?

In concrete coffins his spirit died
The moving pictures froze his might
On electrons his will dispersed
Lost in the silicon wilderness.

Wait! I see a single spark
Defiant in the gathering dark;
From soil and tears
From rivers and leaves
From bricks and rubber
From wires of copper
From wireless webs
From zeros, ones, and logic gates
From memories lost and memories stored
From love, ecstasy, and loss of hope
From crushing sorrow and endless regret
From meaningless chatter and words that matter
From quiet times all too rare,
The spark grows warm
The spark grows strong
Yes it's true but I don't know how—
A light is born! A light is born!

I see him now, rising up
Casting off the flab of years,

His shining eyes a perfect blue
Thunder crowns his head anew.

Forgetting what I want or not
I clang and shake my rusted chains
I promise myself to this newborn god
Daring once more to hope again.

The Sutradhar Speaks

On a scarlet evening in late autumn
Dadhichi opened his eyes
To find Purandara standing before him.

Rishi Dadhichi Speaks

Have you found forgiveness, Purandara?
Are you strong now?
Have you become Indra again?

Purandara Speaks

I now know, O Sage,
Why you had sent me on this quest.

For long did I seek the Ashvins,
Far and wide did I search,
Yet, by failing to understand the true nature of my task
I failed to find the twins.

It was not forgiveness I needed,
But purpose.

My strength would return
When I truly understood
Once more,
The truth of my existence
In the grand order of things;
When I would feel,
Once more, with my entire being,
The weight of my responsibilities,
The bliss of their expectations.

The truth I found was *Bharata.*

Yes, In *Bharata* I found the truth
And within that truth, my purpose.

Every atom, within the divine boundaries
Created by the the sacred network
Of holy *Kshetras* –
The *Shakti Peethas,*
The *Jyotirlingas,*
The *Divya Desams,*
The *Vana Devatas,*
The *Grama Devatas,*
The *KaalaBhairavas,*
The *Tirthas* known and unknown,

And the cremation grounds,
Is *BharataVarsha*;
The *Idea of Bharata*
Is indivisible and irreducible.

This azure sea,
Shining like a carpet of crystals under the Sun-
That destiny of rivers is *Bharata*.

Those emerald fields,
Grain laden stalks rippling in the wind-
That awaiting harvest is *Bharata*.

The snow-capped peaks,
Father of the rivers running wild with freedom-
Their gift of rebirth is *Bharata*.

This earth my hands grasp
Yellow, brown, red, black and everything else-
This soil life giving is *Bharata*.

The rains which drench me
The winds carrying pollen
The tides and the storms
The shimmering haze of summer
The butterfly drinking the morning dew
The fallen leaves under the tree
The mirror-like lotus pond

Reflecting the twinkling stars of the Milky Way
The deer drinking its waters
The tiger lying in wait
The grasshopper jumping on the tips of wet grass –
All of nature is *Bharata*.

Man and woman beside the fire is *Bharata*.
The laughter of children is *Bharata*.
The birth of new life
The passing of those whose time had come
The sound of the temple bell
The majesty of the great dams
Sword soaked in blood
The plough in the ground
Electrons hitting silicon
The glowing lights
All the Raagas
Fervent whispers and passionate speeches
Heartbreaks and betrayals
The first love,
And the ones after that
All of humanity and their civilizations
Is *Bharata*.

The *Aaryas* are *Bharata*.
The Ashvins are *Bharata*.
Varuna is *Bharata*.
Agni is *Bharata*.

Vayu is *Bharata*.
Yama is *Bharata*.
Kubera is *Bharata*.
Indra is *Bharata*.
All *Devatas* are *Bharata*.
I am *Bharata*,
And as *BharataVarsha*,
I shall slay the Serpent
And free the world
From the dark shadow of Ahi.

Life on this earth
Grows ever more pitiful.
How can I be free of debts,
As long as the world itself
Suffers the results of my crimes?

So, in your presence, O *Rishi*,
I renounce all thoughts of redemption.
Accepting the burden of my deeds
I surrender myself at Narayana's feet
Seeking refuge only in my *Karma*.

Take this offering, Dadhichi Atharvan,
Sacred waters from my travels,
Collected from the countless secret streams
Which, defiant till the end
Flow hidden beyond Vritra's gaze,

And, as champions of life
Sustain all that is *Bharata* –
This luminous land,
Broken, yet unbowed before the almighty Ahi
Its bedrock battered but refusing to crumble
Held together by instincts beyond all understanding.

With you as my witness,
I touch this nectar to take my oath-
Bharata is my strength,
Bharatiya is my identity,
BharataVarsha I shall protect.

Rishi Dadhichi Speaks

You have finally understood.
Now you are ready.
Now you have become Indra again.

Indra Speaks

Yet there is a final problem to solve.

How do you free someone
Who does not know they are enslaved?

Starved of knowledge by the *Kaleyas*,
The world today

Does not even know of Vritra
And the harm he has unleashed.

Why would they heed my call?
Why would they unite?

Without humanity awakening to *Dharma*
Even if I slay Vritra alone,
Would he not simply be reborn
Again and again,
As the *Karma* of our corruption?

Rishi Dadhichi Speaks

In that case,
You will have to make them see!

Purandara Speaks

How, O *Rishi*?
I do not understand!
How would I fulfil Vishnu's wishes?
Oh, why do you smile?

Rishi Dadhichi Speaks

Take heart, Indra!
You have almost solved this riddle.

Once the time comes,
Guided by the hand of destiny,
You will find a way-
As long as you stay on the path.

Now, listen to me closely,
As I reveal to you
The Will of Narayana.

Vritra can only be defeated
By the supreme weapon
Which stands on the four legs of *Dharma*-
Tapa, *Shaucha*, *Daya*, and *Satya*,
Austerity, Purity, Kindness, and Truth.

But no such weapon exists today.

For the sake of all the three worlds
I shall give up my body
And merge my *Aatman* with the infinite.
Through the power of my *Yoga*,
I have focused my store of austerities
To harden my skeleton.
These bones are my gift to you,
And through you,
To all life.
Collect them, O Indra!
Take my remains to Tvashta, the *Maker*,

Ask him to use my spine
To forge the *Vajra*,
That awesome armament
Which can be wielded
Only by a Yogi
Submitted completely to truth.

Brandishing that *Vajra*,
You shall challenge the Great Serpent,
And then accept the judgement of destiny.

We must proceed quickly now
Before my dearest wife returns from the forest.
Let us spare her,
That innocent one,
Still unaware
Of the life she carries in her womb,
The gruesome sight of my passing.

The Sutradhar Speaks

Smiling,
The great sage closed his eyes
Shutting himself off
From Indra's protestations.

The wind stopped blowing.
The water stopped flowing.

The clouds stopped in the sky.
Birds and animals surrounded the hermitage
Alongside weeping masses
Of *Apsaras, Gandharvas*, and *Vidyadharas*.
A lion and a tiger walked in;
Sitting by his side, they roared in unison.
The great Garuda descended from *Vaikuntha*,
To bow down in front of the *Asvattha* tree.
The mountain-like Nandi arrived from *Kailasa*,
Followed by countless ghosts
Blowing conches and rattling the *damaru*.
Pure white swans circled above
Showering Dadhichi with shining *BrahmaKamala*.
The seven great sages arrived from the stars
To chant hymns for the welfare of all.

Just before the sun finally set,
The sound of OM reverberated from all directions.
The body of *Dadhichi Atharvan* burst into flames.
A great emptiness
Entered the hearts of all who watched
The fire reduce that mortal body to ash.

Only the white-hot bones remained.

Indra poured on himself
The waters from the streams of *Bharata*;
He picked up the remains of Dadhichi,

And carrying them on his head,
Began his journey towards the Himalayas.

When Suvarchas returned from the forest,
She found the hermitage empty;
The wind had scattered the ashes of her husband
Among the fallen leaves of autumn.

Alone she stood
By the burnt, black spot
Dotted with still smouldering embers
Under the night shadow of the lonely *Asvattha* tree,
When she felt for the very first time
A light kick from the one within her being,
Finally realising the true sacrifice
That her husband and Indra had extracted from her.

PART SIX

REVOLUTION

The Sutradhar wears a mask of
saffron streaked with vermillion.

1| DECISIONS AND REGRETS

The Sutradhar Speaks

High up in the Himalayas,
Two frozen figures
Sat side by side in a snowstorm
Amidst the ruins of an abandoned hermitage.

A white blizzard was raging
When Indra arrived there.

In front of the silent stare of Tvashta and Virochana
Indra stood,
A steaming spectre,
Holding the bones of Dadhichi
Which melted the ice with its energy
Turning the tempest into lashing rains.

A whisper echoed across the emptiness –
Murderer. Murderer. Murderer.

Murderer
Whispered Tvashta.
Murderer
Whispered Virochana.

Indra Speaks

Deservedly,
The world today knows me by my infamy.

It is the truth I cannot run away from;
Yes, the murderer of your son
Stands before you now.
Yes, my guilt is absolute.

But what about you, Tvashta?
What about your boundless thirst for revenge
Which unleashed the horror of Vritra upon the world?

Virochana Speaks

Spare me the whataboutery, wretch!
Where was this morality,
When you murdered my child in cold blood?
Where was this concern,
When you were butchering the *Asuras*?
Your uncontrolled lust
Destroyed the lives of countless mortals;
Now, when you have lost your power,
Like a hypocrite
You suddenly remember *Dharma*?

We will not forgive you;
May you suffer till the *KaalaChakra* stops spinning.

Indra Speaks

I do not seek forgiveness, Mother.

Neither do I seek atonement,
Nor any redemption.

I willingly submit myself to your judgement,
To suffer all the punishment due and more,
For every crime tied to my name.

I expect no mercy.

The truth is this –
I am not here for myself
But to fulfil my duty,
Which I myself had long forgotten;
On behalf of the suffering world
I have come to beg your husband
For an aid only he can provide.

Tvashta Speaks

What is it that you seek from me?

Indra Speaks

I have with me the bones of Dadhichi *Atharvan*
The *Rishi* who made a supreme sacrifice
The likes of which have never been seen.
Taking pity on the state of the world
He performed the ultimate duty

By giving up his body
So that you could forge the *Vajra* from his bones
With which I may smite Ahi
And release the waters he has kept hostage.

Virochana Speaks

You are asking my husband
To make a weapon for you
So that you may kill our youngest child,
Having already slain our eldest?

Indra Speaks

Is he really your child anymore, Mother?
Does he remember you as father, Tvashta?
Deep in your hearts
You both know that this being,
Born of your hatred for me
And your desire for vengeance
Was infected in its very conception
By the ever-present *Adharma* of our times.

Look down from this desolate peak,
Witness yourself the rampant corruption
Which suffocates the three worlds;
The suffering of life,
The collapse of Order,

The narrowing of minds –
Such is the harvest of the drought,
The gift of your Great Serpent.

Is this the suffering which you wish for, Tvashta?
Is there no one in the world
That you care for enough
To spare them
The horrors of the Age of Vritra?

Virochana Speaks

The men and the *Devatas*
Are one and the same;
The *Adharma* which rules this age
Is the failure of mortal and immortal alike;
Humanity cannot pass the blame
To escape its punishment.

Your sins, Indra,
Are not yours alone.
Indeed, trapped in the human gaze,
You behaved just as they do
Even as they did the same, just like you;
At the first taste of power,
You both succumbed to the delusion
That you were above consequences.

Well, now you finally understand –
Consequences are real.

Tvashta Speaks

And what will you do, Indra,
Once you have killed another son of mine?

Indra Speaks

I shall await judgement, *Maker*,
Along with the rest of humanity.

The Sutradhar Speaks

The hills and the valleys echoed with the Maker's chant.

At a gesture from Tvashta,
The bones of Dadhichi rose up;
Guided by the mind of the *Maker*
They began to rearrange themselves
In an intricate pattern
Which no eye could fathom.

The air grew charged and heavy
Pregnant with barely restrained violence –
Faster and faster the bones whirled,

Drawing unto them
The powers of the five elements.

The mountainside cracked
Imbuing the relic with the strength of Earth,
Water emerged from a bottomless fissure
To cleanse the bones and make them pure,
Using the Fire of his own body
Tvashta gave the weapon its terrible form,
And finally,
Starlight descended from the outer realms,
Granting that weapon life and will;
And thus *Vajra* was born.

When that immense *Vajra*
Settled down on the ground,
The Goddess of the Earth cried out in pain;
Oppressed by its overwhelming energy
Her convulsions became earthquakes.

Controlling his senses,
Indra picked up that writhing armament;
Raising it skyward
He bound the *Vajra* to himself,
With tendrils of lightning
And his very own breath,
Promising the ten directions
To bear the pain of that weapon
Until the very end of time.

Virochana Speaks

Foolish husband!
You have been deceived,
By that eternal deceiver, Indra.
Heartless father!
How could you make that terrifying weapon
Which will cause the death
Of yet another son of yours
By the hands of the criminal *Devatas*?

Tvashta Speaks

I suddenly remembered three young birds
Who called me grandfather;
They were born out of the body of *Vishvarupa.*
They flew away
When I was immersed in grief
And consumed by rage.

Will they not be suffering now, wife?
Is it not time for us to look ahead?

The Sutradhar Speaks

Silently,
Virochana left for Mount Meru,
Her fists clenched,
Her dry eyes flashing with rage.

Tvashta turned around,
Alone once more
And trudged the other way;
When the blizzard stopped,
Two sets of footsteps froze,
Forever in opposite directions.

Only Indra remained
Standing very, very still,
Yet pulsing with energy,
Alone in that ravaged hermitage
Back to where it had all begun.

2| ON THE BRINK

The Sutradhar Speaks

Drawn out by the power of his *Vajra*,
The senses returned to Indra,
One by one –
As if waking up from a long dream,
Yet somehow sharper than ever before.

Along with his senses, returned his perception;
The anguished cry of innocents
The pangs of hunger of the poor
The stench of all-pervasive corruption
The caustic poison in the air –
Each one a hammer blow
Hitting Indra all at once
Until at last the floodgates opened
Revealing in garish detail
The true horror of reality.

With newfound clarity,
Indra saw Vritra for what he truly was –
Not just a spirit of vengeance
Not just a reaction to *Adharma*,
But the very incarnation of *Avidya*,
The primordial un-knowledge that is the source of
Chaos.

The malevolence of the Great Serpent
Oozed out from the top of Mount Meru
Enmeshing the world
In its corrosive embrace;
Like the roots of a banyan tree
That venom of ignorance
Connected Ahi to all of existence,
One life at a time.

Yes, every single living being was tied to Vritra.
Even Indra.
Even the Devatas.
Even you and me.

Seduced by the venom of Vritra,
We forget who we are,
Letting our instincts become our master –
We all become *Kaleya*,
Turning into our own oppressor,
Our bond with Vritra grows ever stronger,
In turn strengthening the Great Serpent.

Stunned by that horrifying vision,
Indra could not fathom
Where Vritra ended and where Life began.

Was there truly any difference
Between Vritra and the world he tormented?

On whom should Indra cast his *Vajra*?
On the Great Serpent?
On the Life that sustained his terror?
On both?
On himself?
Or was this the nature of Life itself,
To be embraced and accepted?

Perhaps the apocalypse was the only escape remaining…

Three birds,
Fully grown,
Their feathers tinged with gold,
Landed in front of Indra.

"*We bring a message from Brihaspati,*" said Tittiri.
"*Your strength is not in your arms,*" said Kalapinga.
"*Break down your cage,*" said Kapinjala.
"*You cannot look back,*" said all three,
And then flew away.

Indra watched their golden shimmer
Follow the frozen footsteps of Tvashta;
Now, only one final deed remained
Before he could challenge Vritra again.

The King of the *Devatas* repaired the altar of Trishira-
The same one he had himself destroyed

On the day of his *Mahapaap*,
So many monsoons ago.

He struck the altar with a lightning bolt.

Thus igniting the frozen ground
He cut himself open;
By offering drops of his own blood
He invited Agni in the manner of kings.

Agni arrived after a while;
Famished,
Pale,
Unhealthy and unheated,
A cold fire
Barely a spark,
Barely visible.

Indra Speaks

Though it grieves me, old friend,
To see you thus bereft of splendour,
Now is not the time to lament what is
But to strive instead
Towards an impossible hope.

Sage Dadhichi, with iron will,
Made the supreme sacrifice
To grant us his divine remains;

Tvashta the *Maker* held back his tears and anger
To fashion this *Vajra* from those immortal bones.

Yet, when I grasped this weapon,
It led me to an epiphany
That I too was to be an instrument
Just like the *Vajra* I hold in my hands.

The Great Serpent born of Tvashta's vengeance
Is no mere beast,
But chaos incarnate,
The inverse of *Rta*.

When life will call out to life,
When life will seek harmony with life
When the tapestry that binds mortals with immortals
Be resplendent once again
So that no one is above
And no one is below
When the *Aaryas* would remember who they are,
Only then the *Kaleyas will* be defeated,
Only then will Vritra finally fall.

That is the task of the *Devatas*,
That is why we all must return.

I need your help,
Lord of the Flames.

Even in this frail state
You still are the primordial witness –
Nothing remains hidden from you;
Go and give out the call,
Bring the *Devatas* here
Let them reveal themselves
And inspire humanity once again.

Agni Speaks

I am much too weak,
Much too hungry;
I do not know where the *Devatas* are, O King!
After the fall of *Svarga*
They hid in their elements,
Their diminished forms too weak
To stand against the gaze of Vritra.

From the pyramids to the V8
From the inquisition to credit cards
From the printing press to the world wide web
From broiler chickens to the moon rockets
From the Wall Street to the Kalashnikov
From the Black Death to the refrigerator
In neon lights and gleaming screens
In content clouds and livestreams
In endless scrolls and cancelled fates
In nothing-you-will-own and private jets,

The *Devatas* saw humanity flourish and prosper-
Blissfully unaware,
Unconcerned of consequences,
Contentment their enemy,
Happiness and sorrow reduced to chemical imbalance
Truth, an unbearable stigma to their tailored worlds,
Whipped on by invisible hands from the moment of
their birth
Relentlessly in pursuit
Of the seductive mirage of grow, grow grow –
Willingly losing themselves
Inside the inescapable labyrinth of unfulfillment
Constructed by Vritra and the ghastly *Kaleyas.*

If they had asked me,
I would have told them one simple truth –
When the kindling runs out
So does the fire,
But in the age of *everything is possible*
To speak of limits and consequences
Is to earn the disdain of men
And court the hatred of women.

Left behind without a thought,
The immortals remain trapped today
In the umbra beyond the human gaze,
Cocooned in neglect
Hurt and forgotten

Yet waiting to be reborn,
On the day the spirits of men will grasp for hope again,
And you, O King, will give the call
For the *Devatas* to finally return home.

But first it is you who must free yourself,
Discard the cage that binds you –
By your own strength,
Break out of the human gaze
Become once more freedom incarnate,
The awe-inspiring symbol of purest consciousness.

Manifest your lightning to shatter all that is dark,
Unleash howling winds on the grasslands
Pummel the fields with driving rain
Let your thunderclap silence the metropolis.

Return.

Let your power destroy the citadels of Vritra,
Those very institutions
Which, hidden in plain sight,
Keeps the world mired in delusion,
Churning out the hordes of *Kaleyas*
To enforce Vritra's dark reality
In the name of enlightened progress.

Let the flames of their burning strongholds
Reveal your form to the mortals and immortals alike;

Let both of them remember who they are
So that they too can break free
From the endless grip of Ahi.

The Sutradhar Speaks

So Shakra took to the skies.

In furious anger,
Indra descended upon the demonic *Kaleyas*,
Shattering bones and stones
With pillars of lightning unleashed from the *Vajra*.

With every thunder strike,
Indra, and all the rest of the living,
Felt their link to Vritra
Convulse with unbearable agony.

The citadels of Kaleyas were like forts and gardens
Some were like courts and schools,
Others like stages and markets,
Like brothels and presses,
Or even homes and assemblies,
Yet the unsparing lightning of Indra
Destroyed their *Maya* once and for all
To reveal their true face to all who could see –
Corruption.

Indra Speaks

O Agni!
Hear my call!
Accept this offering!
Feast on these chains that enslave humanity!
Burn them to the ground,
And become bright!
Let your flames reveal the truth of Vritra to the world!

You are the witness!
Let everyone see the state of this earth!

LET
EVERYONE
SEE.

The Sutradhar Speaks

One by one,
The strongholds encircling *Jambudvipa* fell,
All ninety-nine of them,
And like ninety-nine pyres they burned.

Agni entered them,
Agni consumed them,
Agni became a blazing flame
Which turned the skies red.

In the light cast by that garland of fire
The horrific form of Vritra
Coiled atop Mount Meru
Was seen by every mortal eye
In the three worlds.

The sight of the raging Vritra
Shattered all their illusions;
In that flaming night,
All colours seeped out from the world.

When they realized
How utterly weak,
How utterly fragile,
How utterly transient,
All that they held dear truly was –
All the mortals finally awoke
To the core truth of their existence.

No, they were not free.
No, they were not in control.
No, they were not secure.
No, they did not have a choice.

And when the mortals saw
This true condition of their lives
Their minds collapsed.

The doors of Chaos opened.

Vritra began to laugh.

The world fell silent.
Indra's voice echoed across the emptiness
Frantic,
Desperate,
Increasingly hopeless.

LET
EVERYONE
SEE.

It was time for the *Devatas* to return.

3| A RITUAL OF CHANGE

The Sutradhar and the Voices Unseen Speak

It was Sarama who first answered Indra's call.
The lost hound,
Tracking her master's voice,
Found the way back
To once again run beside Purandara.

Then rose Airavata;
The many-headed white elephant
Seemed like the flying mountains of yore
Whose wings were once clipped by Indra himself.

When Indra ascended his mount
He became visible to mortal eyes.
The iridescent spectre of Indra's effulgence
Shone blindingly bright atop the giant Airavata;
When the King of *Devatas* raised his *Vajra*,
Rumbling and dark the storm clouds swirled
Whipped on by the raging howls of Sarama.

Ahi spread his wings;
Glinting aureate to the flashes of lightning,
Draped in flowing black fumes
Sprawled atop his shattered peak
He growled and snarled
And mocked and laughed

At the world which he had once
Mercifully allowed to forget the dread of his gaze.

On either end of the horizon
Loomed the smouldering forms of Vritra and Indra –
Facing each other across the churning sky
Titanic,
Barely restrained,
The world below their quivering battleground.

This is my earliest memory of this life.

Our senses returned,
And we mortals feared Indra;
Thinking he was the greater fiend,
We dared not look up –
We crawled in dread,
And we shut our eyes,
For the sight of a *Devata* is too terrible an ordeal
To be faced by an untrained mind.

But there was to be no turning back.

Through his violence and his force
Indra kept feeding Agni
The flesh of the Age of Vritra;
The earth was soon covered by a dome of flames.

The Ashvin twins awoke to Indra's violence.

From the deepest refuge of humanity,
They emerged to comfort the living.
Every mortal found them by their side,
Even me;
I drank the elixir they gave me,
And we spoke at length of things mundane
Until slowly I felt my strength return
Alongside the courage to open my eyes.

And those of us who were scared
And those of us in hiding
And those of us without hope –
All felt the pull of Indra's call
To look up in spite of ourselves
Compelled by an urge beyond my understanding
Seeking what I did not know.

So I looked up.

The sky of fire carried the call of Indra
Uncaring,
Insistent,
Chain breaking
Pulling me up when I was so used to lying prone
Searching,
Seeking,
Squeezing
The last vestiges of my most primal instincts.

All pretensions went away.
Correct and incorrect became meaningless.
Feelings were replaced by awareness.
We scrambled,
We clawed in the mud,
We thrashed about,
Gritting our teeth
Willing ourselves to break free
Until finally,
Ugly, covered in dirt and sweat,
The mortals finally stood up.

I finally stood up.

Still unused to stand on our own
We grasped each other for balance
Tottering on the brink of another fall;
Fear stalked our wobbling mass,
Sniffing, salivating,
Waiting for the precise moment to pounce
And destroy us forever.

Then we saw grim faced Varuna emerge from the waters.

Twirling his fearsome noose
He growled softly;
The fear fled.
Varuna clasped the hands of the mortals,

Oh yes, he clasped my hand,
As he had clasped yours too –
Do you not remember?
His waters washed away the slippery mud,
His salt brought us back to awareness.
With steady feet we mortals stood.

Water, salt and the hand that holds –
To each one of us Varuna gave these gifts
And then put his noose around our necks
As though to remind us, if ever we forget,
The value of law
The value of oaths
The value of brotherhood;
Thus did we receive once again
The three building blocks of civilization,
Secured by the threat of Varuna's promise –
The inevitability of just punishment for crimes.

The world is not meaningless.
Not unless we make it so.

No longer struggling to stand,
I felt the warmth of the roaring Agni,
I saw his towering flames
Devour the havoc wrought by Indra
Burning ever brighter
To unveil my broken world with pitiless clarity.

We all heard Vayu whisper in our ears
"The time is now.
Come, break your bonds.
Come, let us fight Vritra.
Come, let us tame the uncaring Chaos.
Come, let us reclaim life."

The Devatas returned.

I saw them with my own two eyes.

The Devatas returned;
And so did hope.

With hope,
Came remembrance –
Of the *Wisdom of Honey* shared long back,
Of a reality where goodness was possible,
Of a reality we had given up as lost.

We remembered that we were *Aarya*
Bound by the threads of life to every living being
None of us alone
All of us, a *forest.*

When we awoke as *Aarya,*
The *Kaleyas* fled.

As *Aaryas* we marched out –
The jungles emptied.
The villages emptied.
The cities emptied.
The waters emptied.
Every living being sought out Indra;
Our gathering of souls became a crowd,
The crowd became an uprising,
The uprising became a nation,
And that nation was *Bharata*,
And as *Bharata* we took a vow
To reforge the sacred bond
Between the mortals and the immortals
To safeguard *all* life,
To walk once more the *Way of the Aarya*.

Slowly, *Airavata* began his march across the sky
Led by the bounding *Sarama*,
We the living followed him,
Dancing with joy
In the sky, in the air and on ground
Waving our freedom as our flags;
Drunk on the memory of *Honey*
Bharata finally became a *Yatra*.

We marched to the centre of the world
To the shattered peaks of Mount Meru,
Where Vritra lay in wait.

Like a tidal wave,
That mass of life surged forward
From all corners of the earth
All of us *Bharata*,
All of us *Yatri*;
When we stepped over the fallen citadels
The ground flattened beneath our feet-
We left a clean slate waiting behind us.

Around the mountain we gathered
Restless and excited,
Heaving and clamouring –
Ah! What a glorious confusion it was,
Full of meaning!
Each one of us felt our power,
Each one of us challenged Vritra,
We shook our fists at the Meru,
Thinking we were Indra ourselves.

Yes.
We were Indra ourselves.
We were all Indra.
All of us
Indra
Standing up to our very own Vritra.

Driven by our roars
Airavata charged at Meru,

Again and again,
Ignoring the blinding torrent of his own blood
Each impact a deafening earthquake;
The mountain shook,
Cracks appeared on its sides
The ground broke into black chasms
Until slowly, oh so slowly,
The great body of Meru began to tilt.

A great shadow then fell on the gathered host,
A voice answered from beyond the clouds
Mocking us in delight
Like the distant sound of rumbling thunder
Creeping ever closer, forever,
Yet denying rain to the parched earth.

Vritra Speaks

Indra.

Finally you have come, tyrant.
Finally, what I was born to accomplish,
Has been achieved through your efforts.

Now comes that part of the story
Where resolution happens simply
Through pure strength,
And the violence it grants.

Come on now!
Do not look so disappointed!

Is this not the truest end
Shorn of all the sophistry
Which clouds the vision
Of your dutifully civilized human gaze?

What is more primal, more pure
Than two forces,
Utter opposites
Clashing until the bitter end?

The chaos of the Many,
Until they become Two.
The balance of the Two,
Until they become the One.
The loneliness of the One
Until it becomes Nothing.
From Nothing comes chaos again
Is this not the divine rhythm?
Is this not the most fundamental miracle?
Is this not the beating heart of all creation?

Yet you fools don't see it!
No. You prefer a prison-garden
Of precisely laid out paths
Flanked by topiary morals

Neat and clean, fully labelled –
That is good!
This is bad!
That is the start!
This is the end!
So that you may be excused from thinking
And be permitted to waste your lives,
Clinging on with all your might
To those meaningless stickers.

Ah, how easily you can refuse
The truth shimmering all around you!

Things change.
That is the nature of creation
Its horror
Its beauty
Its wonder
Its ultimate truth.

Let go of your pitiful concerns;
Everything will be destroyed
Whether by your hands or not
Whether you witness it or not
Whether you resist it or not-
If not today, then tomorrow
Or in the endless days stretching beyond the next.

Let go.
Let go.
Let go.
In the end, there is Nothing
Except Nothingness

Then why wait any longer?
Should we not, at this very instant,
Obliterate this horrible Creation
This final remnant, the failed *Devatas*
So useless
So futile
So illusory
So full of suffering?

Come, all you Indras,
Rise up to me,
Let us fight,
Dancing to the rhythms of eternal change,
Let us dare to grasp pure freedom
To seek the ultimate thrill,
Swaying our consciousness
To the pendulum of free will –
From Chaos to Nothingness
From Nothingness to Chaos.

The Sutradhar Speaks

Laughing,

Singing,
Roaring,
Vritra revealed himself
As the dark spectre of a world in flames;
His great wings stretched beyond the horizon
Dripping purple fire into the darkness
His ghastly eyes were ablaze
Terrifying the very stars to flicker in and out of
existence
His endless body serpentine
Choking the earth
As well as the throats of all who beheld his terror.

Many perished,
Unable to bear the sudden emptiness in their chests
Those of us who didn't lost their power to feel
Until a single bolt of white lightning
Rose up defiant and bright;
Crackling with power
It banished the reek from the monster.

Indra and Vritra clashed amidst the ruins of *Svarga*.

Like an intricate dance
They moved in unison
Each seeking an opening
To land the first blow.

With his tail
And his talons
And his poison
And his scales,
Vritra created a grand confusion,
His movements a blur to the naked eye.

Yet Indra kept his focus,
And when the right moment came
Hurled the *Vajra*,
Striking Ahi on the arm
With the strength of shattering atoms.
The Serpent,
Though stunned for a moment,
Lashed out wildly,
With all his power,
Threatening to rupture the fabric of reality itself.

But Indra was the supreme warrior.
He called the *Vajra* back to himself
And crouching the avoid the tail of Vritra
Struck him on his other arm
Rendering it forever useless.

Vritra fell,
Sliding down the side of Meru
Like an angry gash,
Finally coming to rest in the twilight region of the
Pitri.

Wildly Ahi thrashed about,
Crushing the rocks into fine powder.
His venom darkened all existence,
Spewing out in titanic geysers
From the wounds of his contorted, writhing body,
While he heaved and wailed in agony.

Unforgiving, relentless,
Indra descended like a meteor ablaze;
His *Vajra* became pure lightning
Purple and Blue and Black and White,
Crackling, humming, shuddering
With barely restrained violence.

With a final strike of his weapon,
Indra ended Ahi's torment;
The mountain-like skull of the Great Serpent
Shattered Into countless bloody fragments,
Showering the earth with sizzling gore.

A single triumphant thunderclap rang across the worlds
Followed briefly by an utter silence
And then,
By the chilling noises of hopeless pain.

4| THE LAP OF MY MOTHER

The Sutradhar Speaks

Pain.
Horrifying pain.
Pain, with no end in sight.
The world screamed in pain.
All we could see
All we could hear
All we could feel
Was only an unbearable, overpowering pain
Choking our voices and our minds.

We could not even whimper.

In the distance, we saw Indra
Drenched in Vritra's rainbow blood
Wrapped in the toxic haze of the monster's dying
breath
Frozen
Still
Shackled by the howls of torment that filled the world.

Even the *Devatas* could not withstand
That hellstorm of poison and flesh;
Like everyone else,
They fell to their knees.

The terrible hag of *Brahmahatya*
Arose from the ground;
To extract the price of *Karma*
She grabbed Indra by his throat,
And dragged him across the earth
Diminishing his heroic form into a tornado of dust.

There is neither redemption nor damnation,
Only the inescapable consequences of our actions –
Nothing more, nothing less,
Without exceptions,
Such is the inviolable Law of Karma
Of which we all are subjects.

A deep rumble.

For just one moment,
The space froze around the fallen Meru
As if a horrid curtain to an infernal stage
Parting which the hag reappeared
Now resembling a monstrous mountain;
Smiling at us
She opened her palm
Painted in the deepest red that the mind can imagine
And began to laugh.

A tiny being leapt from her index finger,
Insignificant, powerless,

No bigger than a blade of grass;
Chased by her laughter
That helpless one fled through the sludge
Until it disappeared inside a lake
In whose turgid waters bloomed a single purple lotus.

She then opened her infinite mouth towards us.

"Mercy, Mercy, Mercy."
The world wept in terror.
"Save us, save us, save us."

In that moment of crisis
When the *damaru* of *Pralaya* seemed inevitable
A sixteen-year-old girl
Wearing red
Bedecked in red
Carrying a skull bearing red
Was seen seated on the headless corpse of Vritra.

Laughing with abandon,
She consumed the corpse
Along with the poison
And set fire to the mountain.

The terrible hag faded from our sight.

The *Mahavidyas* appeared,
Floating above the flames

Like a crown above the girl –
Ten suns on a blood-red sky.

"Give us hope,"
The *Devatas* said.
"Give us hope,"
The humans said.
"Give us hope,"
The animals said.
"Give us hope,"
The fishes said.
"Give us hope,"
The plants said.
"Give us hope,"
All life said.
"Give us hope,"
All that is not-life also said.

"Give us hope," I said.

"Give us hope," I heard you say.

"Give us hope," we all said.

"Let knowledge be your hope," we heard back.

Knowledge is hope.
What else is hope?
What else can be hope?

"Yes, Knowledge is our hope", we said.

Then the sky cleared.
The burning Meru fell silent.

With a deafening explosion
The waters burst forth,
Sparkling and clear.

A fragrant white mist,
Flowing down from the mountaintop,
Cleansed us all.

A new birth
A fresh start
A clean slate;
Fragile
Delicate
Beautiful
The perfect centre between Chaos and Nothingness,
Harmony.

We saw a radiant maiden
Clad in saffron and white
Carrying a veena,
Seated on a lotus,
Float down the waters
On the back of a white swan.

It was the coming of spring,
The first dawn of the rest of our lives.

Our speechless voices found speech.

The Age of Knowledge
(*The Aaryas, who are the Voices Unseen*)

Darkness retreats.
A new Sun rises.
Life renews.

O Mother Sarasvati!
The most auspicious,
Lotus-eyed Goddess of Knowledge,
Who is Knowledge,
Grant us Knowledge!

Let this human age flourish.
Let ignorance perish.
Let us worship knowledge.
Let knowledge be our guide.

Let knowledge grant us wisdom.
Let knowledge grant us prosperity.
Let knowledge grant us compassion.
Let knowledge grant us love.

Knowledge is *Dharma*.
Let us find *Dharma* in knowledge,
Through *Dharma* let us be *Aarya*,
As *Aarya*, let us find peace.

Let there be peace.
Let there be peace.
Let there be peace.

The Sutradhar Speaks

I cupped my hands,
And drank the water from that river.

EPILOGUE

The Sutradhar is the familiar stranger in the mirror.

1| THE AGE OF MAN

The Sutradhar Speaks

Thus, Vritra was defeated.
Thus did the Goddess gift us knowledge.

So, what really changed?
Did we find meaning in the world,
Or was the *Way of the Aarya* a mere mirage?

Oh, I know what *happened.*

While Purandara suffered his *Karma*
Imprisoned in a lotus stalk
Surrounded by the azure sheen of a boundless lake
Nahusha the human became Indra.

Wielding the power of the immortals
Proud and arrogant the mortal grew;
Consumed by lust,
Nahusha reached for that which was not his,
And was cast down from *Svarga*,
His body cursed to become a serpent
In a cruel parody of Vritra.

The world grew dry once more
When Agastya drank up the waters
Upon the thoughtless request of the *Devatas*
To reveal the acolytes of Vritra hidden in the seas.

When Kapila burned down the arrogant sons of Sagara
Bhagiratha Ikshvaku did the impossible
For the sake of his sixty thousand ancestors.
By his will and his austerities,
That glorious king won the favour of Shiva
To become the father of Ganga in the realm of the living,
Granting prosperity to earth
And salvation to all her beings.

All this happened
And much, much, much more.

With time, the memory of Vritra faded,
Until it was but a receding shadow
In the unspoken corner of our minds
A vague sand grain of discomfort,
Unacknowledged,
Unspoken, unreal –
Ultimately unthought.

Friend, let me whisper a secret to you –
Time is a spiral
Life does not end
You were here before
And you will be here many times more,
Yet take heart,
Your struggle is not some futile joke.

Civilizations rise and fall.
Everything changes,
Again and again,
Except just this –
In every age, there is a hidden Vritra
In every age, there is a sleeping *Bharata*
In every age, there is a fallen Indra.

You are that Indra,
Your world is that *Bharata*,
Your struggles and your despair,
The shadow of your very own Vritra.

In your hands lie your fate,
In your fate,
The fate of all Creation;
What will you choose, my friend –
Will you rise?
Will you awaken?
Will you slay?
Will you become an *Aarya*?
Or, will just let things be
Wandering aimlessly in all your lives and deaths
Moving ever further away from blissful liberation?

As in the world
So within you,
As within you
So in the world.

2| MEMORIES FROM ANOTHER LIFE

The Sutradhar Speaks

I once believed,
That I was the hero of my own story;
So, I left home
Just like I imagined heroes did.

The journey was long.
Driven by flaming ardour
I did not stray
(or so I thought, out of breath);
I left blood steps on thorny tracks
I drank sweat-water on desert dunes
I punched handholds on sheer cliffs
I forced my carcass ever upwards
An inch at a time,
Gasping under the invisible weight
Of all the baggage holding me back.

Proud, proud, proud I was.

Refusing to look back,
I unburdened recklessly
Cutting off pieces of myself
One by one;
Scarcely caring what I kept and what I lost –
I shed,
Becoming lighter.

Rising,
Diminishing,
Succeeding,
Looking always, always ahead
Until I found myself
At the very top of the mountain;
There was nothing else left to achieve.

Drunk with the mead of triumph
Ears ringing with faceless cheers
Ritually hugging queued-up strangers,
I ascended a well-worn throne,
Beautiful and inviting to my believing eyes
As if it had been waiting just for me.

I told myself I deserved this;
Success, love, adulation.
Had I not travelled?
Had I not worked hard?
Had I not unburdened?
Had I not shed, lightened, and diminished?
Had I not always looked ahead?
Who else but me deserved this?

I grasped the throne with all my might
And laid claim to the world below,
Smug in my exalted perch.

"I have won."

Then the tremors came.
Then the lightning struck.
Perhaps in hindsight,
Inevitable.
But how was I to know then?

My world shattered into countless broken dreams.

The sizzling ruins of my grand hubris
My precious palimpsest of success
Disappeared before my maddened gaze
Like mist escaping through clenched fists.

The throne never existed.
The strangers were, in fact, strangers.
The mountaintop was an illusion.
The world was not mine.

I…
I was alone.
The world was *Maya*.

I fell.

The blurry ground
Barely visible from my imaginary perch
Left behind, disdained and forgotten
Once so distant

So dreamlike
Swiftly came back into sharp focus
As I passed through the clouds.
Real.
All too real.

Layers of my blindfold peeled away.

Memories flooded back,
Accompanied by spectres of Not-Strangers.
Spectres with faces,
Names I knew,
All of them witnesses of my vaunted climb
The very same one which made them Strangers,
And now,
Susurrant spectators to my fall.

Down, all the way down I fell,
Till I crashed into the undergrowth
Reaching the very bottom of the world.

The swaying canopies
Over which I once soared proud,
Cast a liminal net of light and shadow
Strangely hypnotic,
On my broken mortal frame.

In that nameless forest
I lay on my back,

Unblinking, utterly spent
My body scarred with pinpricks of disapproval;
No, disappointment,
Or perhaps even more painful,
Indifference,
From those who I pretended to care for
And those who cared for me,
Lives I had taken for granted
As mere stepping stones
In my self-righteous, self-absorbed march.

Shamelessly,
With a pathetic smile on my face
I gave up,
Resigning myself to my fate.

A shroud of silence descended on me,
Comforting my loneliness,
Yet I could not but imagine
The faint whispers of the treetops
Gently murmuring their mirth-
So far, so very far away from home.

"You have nothing.
You are nothing."

I was once on a boat
Floating past burning pyres

Photographing the thick smoke
As it merged with the morning mist.

The pale *Agrahayana* light shimmered,
Playing hide and seek with the gentle wind
Infused with incense, sandalwood, and vermillion
Bearing countless prayers to Ma Ganga
To the chimes of the temple bells of Kashi.

The everlasting fire of the *Manikarnika*
Grew smaller on the horizon
As our boat drifted farther from focus
On the inexorable current of the river.

I shivered when I heard a sudden whisper –
"You shall return here,
And burn."

I had built my life
To forget those words –
The most primal truth
Imprinted within us.

"Nothing lasts;
You will become ash
Along with everything else."

I had armoured my mind
With purpose and goals

To protect myself from those uncontrolled thoughts;
Yet the truth kept flaring
Like an irritating whack-a-mole,
Suddenly, when least expected
An inexplicable emptiness below my chest
Cold sweat on sleepless nights
Terrifying clarity on sleepwalking days.

Now, after my fall,
Those very words
Once a grim reminder
Of remorseless, omnipresent, inevitable,
All-consuming Time,
Returned to me,
Sudden and unbidden.

"I am done.
It is time to say goodbye."

I closed my eyes,
Finally ready to submit to the flames of *Manikarnika*
Until I heard that same whisper once more,
Like a thunderclap on a winter morning-

"Not yet.
You have a story to tell."

NAIMISHARANYA

Does he know that I am here?

His closed eyes were barely visible amidst the millennia thick overgrowth that covered his body. His white beard touched the ground, even though the branch of the banyan tree from which he was hanging must have been at least thirty feet high. I felt a strange sense of peace, here in front of the altar and the ascetic, inside this tiny enclave of the aeons old Naimisha forest.

Naimisharanya. The forest of power, where every tree is a story.

A gibbous moon rose, as if existing only for this extraordinary refuge amongst the swirling Chaos. The musical rustle from the gently swaying branches accompanied the staccato beats of the cackling flames. Something moved. A shining green serpent slithered across the body of the ascetic, and bit him between the eyes. Both of them shuddered as venom mixed with blood, but then the snake went limp and lost her lustre; life fed on life.

Completely drained, the reptile fell down into the altar, the sizzle of burning meat merging into the symphony of the forest. The black fingers of the sage started to move in practised patterns, his mouth wordlessly chanting the language of *Dharma*. A tiny bit of a *Soma* root emerged between the gnarled fingernails – he began to mash it with both hands.

The ten sisters are serving you, Soma,
They have grasped you firmly.
Flow pure, sweet Soma,
Bringer of happiness,
Repeller of foes.

As the colourless liquid started to drip onto the charring snake, the air inside the enclave grew heavy. Unseen voices joined in as the whispering chant grew resonant in power.

In the beginning, He emerged from the Golden Egg,
The Lord of all that is created and uncreated,
To Whom shall we offer our oblation?
To Him shall we offer our oblation.

The fire blazed forth from the altar like an explosion of dawnlight.

He strengthens our souls,
His words the Devatas obey,
His shadow falls on life and death,
To Whom shall we offer our oblation?
To Him shall we offer our oblation.

Tiny floating sparks, dancing above the altar, turned into fireflies and began to trace the contours of a shape – and yet, just as the chants reached a crescendo, a cold wind blew in, sweeping away that which was unformed and that which was forming. Glowing embers got stuck to the flesh of the hanging sage – the stink of burning flesh overpowering the delicate fragrance of the blooming *ketaki* flowers.

The ritual failed.
Again.
The Devatas did not answer.
Again.
The offering was lacking.

Many years ago, at the very conjunction of the declining Dvapar and the ascendant, malevolent Kali, this forest, no – this very same altar, was witness to an epoch-defining incident. Krishna Dwaipayana Ved Vyasa composed The Jaya, which told the story of the Great War, fought among the descendants of the Kuru clan and involving all known and unknown heroes of Aryavarta. His student Vaishampayana recited this in the great Snake Sacrifice of King Janamejaya. The learned Ugrashravas, also known as Sauti, son of the poet Romaharshana, recounted the latter to the Sage Saunaka and his disciples. This narration, which came to be known as the Mahabharata, would serve as a beacon of righteousness in the onrushing darkness that was to descend upon this planet. At least, such was the hope.

The Goddess brought me here.

She picked out my severed head from her garland, and smiled, and blessed me, and placed me by the altar. Her jackal drained my blood.

I was the offering. I am to feed the fire.

As the years passed, this enclave grew more and more remote, until it became a place of legend, far removed from tidings of war and peace, hungrily searched for by bands of storytellers who wandered across the corners of this fractured and desolate countryside. They believed that this had become a special place – the sheer strength of Sauti's narration imbuing it with a mystical power which drew towards itself, like a black hole, all stories told or yet untold. A storyteller's immortality lay in being able to offer his work to this flame. Now it seems that due to that very same power, this forest has been left untouched by the apocalypse, a cosmic refuge reverberating with the power of the Word.

All the threads of all the stories will merge into one, like rivers flowing into the ocean.

I prepared myself for the sacrifice that must be made.

"Accept me," I said.
"Who are you?" the fire asked me back.
"I am a pilgrim. I seek the fire."
"Why do you seek the fire, pilgrim?"
"So that I can get answers."
"I have no answers, pilgrim. I can only burn."
"What will you burn, fire?"
"Everything."
"Will I get my answer then?"

The fire embraced me.
I burned.
I turned to ash.
Carried away by the morning breeze, I became nothing, everywhere.

Farewell, Neighbour.

About the Author

Ratul Chakraborty is one of the most accomplished video-game makers in India. He is fascinated by history and people, the two lenses that form the foundation of his creative perspective.

After more than a decade of procrastination and other assorted excuses, he finally gathered enough courage to take a break from the corporate world in late 2019 and complete writing his highly regarded collection of short stories, *Sutradhar*.

He is the curator of *Shared Roots: Tales from the Indosphere*, an anthology that celebrates the common history and cultural heritage of India and Cambodia.

Ratul loves to travel across India doing street photography and is a lifelong fan of Juventus FC. He is based out of Kolkata, where he lives with his parents, his wife, Surela, and their four-legged daughters Truffles and Mowgli.